Second Edition

Intercultural Communication

Workbook

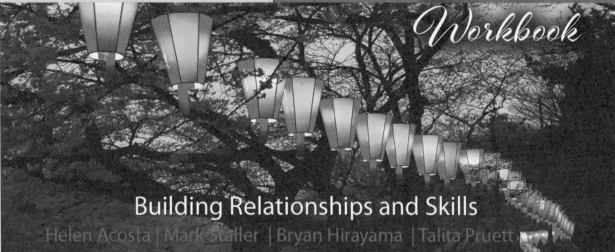

Building Relationships and Skills

Helen Acosta | Mark Staller | Bryan Hirayama | Talita Pruett

Kendall Hunt

publishing company

Kendall Hunt
publishing company

www.kendallhunt.com
Send all inquiries to:
4050 Westmark Drive
Dubuque, IA 52004-1840

Contents

How to Use this Workbook v

Chapter 1   The Foundations of
             Intercultural Communication . . . 1
             Learning Objectives 1
             Workbook Handouts. 1
             Reading Guide 3
             Journal #1 9
             Journal #2 11
             Quiz. 13
             Activity Sheet #1 15
             Activity Sheet #2 17
             Evaluation 21

Chapter 2   Appreciating Both Sameness
             and Difference 23
             Learning Objectives 23
             Workbook Handouts. 23
             Reading Guide 25
             Journal #1 31
             Journal #2 33
             Quiz. 35
             Activity Sheet #1 37
             Activity Sheet #2 39
             Activity Sheet #3 41
             Evaluation 43

Chapter 3   Adaptation and Empathy 45
             Learning Objectives 45
             Workbook Handouts. 45
             Reading Guide 47
             Journal #1 53
             Quiz. 57
             Activity Sheet #1 59
             Evaluation 61

Chapter 4   Verbal Communication 63
             Learning Objectives 63
             Workbook Handouts. 63
             Reading Guide 65
             Journal #1 69
             Quiz. 73
             Activity Sheet #1 75
             Activity Sheet #2 77
             Evaluation 79

Chapter 5   Nonverbal Communication 81
             Learning Objectives 81
             Workbook Handouts. 81
             Reading Guide 83
             Journal #1 89
             Quiz. 95
             Activity Sheet #1 97
             Activity Sheet #2 99
             Evaluation 101

Chapter 6   Approaches to Conflict 103
             Learning Objectives 103
             Workbook Handouts. 103
             Reading Guide 105
             Journal #1 109
             Quiz. 115
             Activity Sheet #1 117
             Evaluation 119

Chapter 7   Values and Worldviews 121
             Learning Objectives 121
             Workbook Handouts. 121
             Reading Guide 123
             Journal #1 131

Journal #2 133
Journal #3 135
Quiz. 139
Activity Sheet #1 141
Evaluation 143

Chapter 8   **History vs. Histories 145**
Learning Objectives 145
Workbook Handouts. 145
Reading Guide 147
Journal #1 151
Journal #2 153
Quiz. 155
Activity Sheet #1 157
Activity Sheet #2 159
Evaluation 161

Chapter 9   **Our Multifaceted**
             Identities. 163
Learning Objectives 163
Workbook Handouts. 163
Reading Guide 165
Journal #1 169
Journal #2 171

Quiz. 175
Activity Sheet #1 177
Activity Sheet #2 179
Evaluation 181

Chapter 10   **Intercultural Communication**
             Across Contexts 183
Learning Objectives 183
Workbook Handouts. 183
Reading Guide 185
Journal #1 191
Journal #2 193
Journal #3 195
Quiz. 197
Activity Sheet #1 199
Activity Sheet #2 201
Activity Sheet #3 203
Activity Sheet #4 205
Activity Sheet #5 207
Activity Sheet #6 209
Activity Sheet #7 213
Activity Sheet #8 217
Evaluation 219

Chapter Quiz Answers 221

How to Use this Workbook

When used in conjunction with your textbook, this workbook is designed to maximize your learning about intercultural communication. For each chapter of your textbook, your workbook provides 1) a checklist of chapter learning objectives and a checklist of workbook handouts, 2) a page for chapter notes, 3) a chapter reading guide, 4) journal assignments, 5) a chapter quiz, and 6) activity sheets. A brief description and explanation of each of these learning aids follows:

1. **Checklist of Chapter Learning Objectives and Workbook Handouts**

   Each section of your workbook begins with a checklist page that lets you keep track of the chapter learning objectives and the workbook handouts for each chapter. Use this page as a guide for understanding the textbook chapter and as a guide for understanding all the resources available to you in your workbook.

   As you complete the workbook handouts for a chapter, you can check off each assignment on this checklist page. (The handout checklist also lists each handout title and page length, so you should find this checklist page very helpful for keeping track of your work.) Once you have completed the workbook handouts, you should be able to check off the chapter learning objectives. If you do not think you have achieved the chapter learning objectives, reread the chapter, redo your work, and/or speak to your instructor.

2. **Chapter Reading Guides**

   The chapter reading guide will help you to comprehend the most important concepts and theories covered in the chapter. Since the reading guide only requires you to read and understand the textbook, it should be fairly easy to fill out. We recommend that you fill out the chapter reading guide first before completing any of the other workbook handouts.

3. **Journal Assignments**

   The journal assignments require a higher level of critical thinking than the chapter reading guides. In order to complete the journal assignments, you will need to make judgments and evaluations, and you will often need to apply the textbook concepts and principles to your own life and your own life experiences. Although the journal assignments are more difficult to complete, they are also more valuable because they provide you with self-knowledge.

4. **Chapter Quizzes**

   Each workbook section contains a two-page chapter quiz. We recommend that you use this quiz as a self-test after you have completed the chapter reading guide and the chapter journal assignments. The quiz answer sheet is located at the back of the workbook. However, try to complete the quiz without looking at the answer sheet in order to discover how much of the chapter material you have mastered.

5. **Activity Sheets**

The activity sheets will give you further practice applying the textbook principles. After you have completed the chapter reading guide, the journal assignments, and the chapter quiz, the activity sheets will help you to develop specific skills and knowledge that will reinforce or supplement your learning.

6. **Chapter Evaluation**

After completing all of the other workbook handouts for each chapter, you are ready for the highest level of critical thinking: evaluating the textbook and what you have (or have not) learned it. Filling out the Chapter Evaluation will help you to become and independent, critical thinker. The Chapter Evaluation will help you to jot down your thoughts about the most difficult or confusing ideas of the chapter, the most controversial or hard to accept ideas of the chapter, suggestions for improving the chapter, the most important or useful ideas from the chapter, and the most important chapter skills and/or attitudes to develop. In order to develop your curiosity, make sure you do not skip "questions generated by reading the chapter."

Chapter 1

The Foundations of Intercultural Communication

Chapter Learning Objectives

(Check off when you think a learning objective has been achieved.)

1. _____ Develop a basic vocabulary related to intercultural communication in order to understand the connection between communication and culture.

2. _____ Gain a deeper understanding of culture by learning the functions of culture, some similes for culture, and some important characteristics of culture.

3. _____ Know the general history of the study of culture and the specific history of Intercultural Communication studies.

4. _____ Understand and appreciate the major reasons to study Intercultural Communication.

5. _____ Learn the essential information one needs to know in order to become more cosmopolitan.

6. _____ Develop the ability to evaluate intercultural communication competence.

Workbook Handouts

(Check off when each handout has been completed.)

_____ Chapter 1 Reading Guide (6 pages)

_____ Chapter 1 Journal #1 (Reasons to Study Intercultural Communication) (2 pages)

_____ Chapter 1 Journal #2 (Intercultural Communication Competence) (2 pages)

_____ Chapter 1 Quiz (2 pages)

_____ Chapter 1 Activity Sheet #1 (Co-Culture Report Sheet) (2 pages)

_____ Chapter 1 Activity Sheet #2 (National Culture Report Sheet) (4 pages)

_____ Chapter 1 Evaluation (2 pages)

Name: _____   Period: _____

ICC Chapter 1 Reading Guide

According to the textbook, what is a human society?

_____

_____

_____

Define the term "culture" according to our textbook:

_____

_____

List AND define the four terms related to culture:

1. _____

_____

2. _____

_____

3. _____

_____

4. _____

_____

What is a cultural artifact?

_____

_____

Explain the difference between indigenous cultures and national cultures:

_____

_____

_____

Explain what deep-structure institutions are: _____

_____

_____

What is the primary social group that transmits and maintains cultural beliefs, values, and behaviors in any society? _____

According to the textbook, what is the definition for religion?

_____

_____

Explain the difference between enculturation and acculturation:

_____

_____

_____

_____

Who creates a dominant culture?

_____

_____

_____

Provide two other names for dominant cultures:

1. _____

2. _____

According to the textbook, what is popular culture?

_____

_____

Provide four examples of popular culture:

1. _____

2. _____

3. _____

4. _____

Explain the difference between a subculture and a co-culture:

_____

_____

_____

Give the textbook definition of the term "communication" :

_____

_____

List AND describe the seven components of communication:

1. _____

2. _____

3. _____

4. _____

5. _____

6. _____

7. _____

Define intercultural communication:

_____

_____

_____

List AND define the five subfields of human communication:

1. _____

2. _____

3. _____

4. _____

5. _____

Explain what is meant by the assertion that human culture would not exist without communication and human communication would not exist without culture:

_____

_____

_____

_____

What is the modern sense of the term "culture" ? _____

_____

_____

List the six different academic areas in which culture is an important concept:

1. _____   4. _____

2. _____   5. _____

3. _____   6. _____

List and describe the major functions of culture:

1. _____

2. _____

3. _____

4. _____

List AND describe the four similes for culture discussed in the textbook:

1. _____

   _____

2. _____

   _____

3. _____

   _____

4. _____

   _____

What are three important characteristics of culture?

1. _____

2. _____

3. _____

When did the study of intercultural communication begin?_____

List 15 reasons to study and care about intercultural communication:

1. _____   8. _____

2. _____   9. _____

3. _____   10. _____

4. _____   11. _____

5. _____   12. _____

6. _____   13. _____

7. _____   14. _____

                    15. _____

In the Greek language, what does the term "cosmopolitan" stand for? _____

_____

_____

List the first four areas of the Cosmopolitan Primer AND provide one fact from each:

1. _____

2. _____

3. _____

4. _____

Provide three actions you could take AND one action you could avoid to become more cosmopolitan:

1. _____

2. _____

3. _____

Avoid: _____

Where is the full American Association of Colleges and Universities VALUE rubric posted?

_____

_____

_____

What three major areas does the Intercultural Effectiveness Scale (IES) by The Kozai Group evaluate?

1. _____

2. _____

3. _____

When comparing the AACU VALUE rubric and the IES, what is the difference between the two?

_____

_____

_____

Name: _____   Period: _____

ICC Chapter 1 Journal #1

Reasons to Study Intercultural Communication

In Chapter 1 of your Intercultural Communication textbook, you learned 15 different reasons why the study and practice of intercultural communication are important:

1. Advances in Transportation Technologies
2. Advances in Communication Technologies
3. Globalization
4. Travel and Tourism
5. Education and Study Abroad
6. Governmental Work and Diplomacy
7. World Peace
8. Social Welfare and Social Justice
9. Immigration and Domestic Diversity
10. Effective Healthcare Communication
11. Communication Between Co-Cultures
12. Enhanced Interpersonal Relationships
13. Increased Sensitivity To Others
14. Increased Self-Awareness
15. Greater Ability To Avoid Embarrassing Situations

List your top five reasons for studying and caring about intercultural communication, and briefly explain why these reasons are most important to you.

#1 Reason: _____

Why important: _____

_____

_____

#2 Reason: _____

Why important: _____

_____

_____

#3 Reason: _____

Why important:_____

_____

_____

#4 Reason: _____

Why important: _____

_____

_____

#5 Reason: _____

Why important: _____

_____

_____

Evaluate how motivated you are about studying intercultural communication (circle one answer):

Not at all motivated.   Not very motivated.   Somewhat motivated.   Very motivated.

Explain your current level of motivation: _____

_____

_____

_____

In addition to studying Intercultural Communication, how do you currently feel about communicating one-on-one with people from other cultures? (Note that you may have "mixed" feelings, both positive and negative.) What are the reasons for your current feelings about communicating one-on-one with people from other cultures?

_____

_____

_____

_____

_____

_____

Do you like the notion of cosmopolitanism? Do you want to become more cosmopolitan? Why or why not?

_____

_____

_____

_____

Name: _____   Period: _____

ICC Chapter 1 Journal #2

Intercultural Communication Competence

The AACU Intercultural Knowledge and Competence Rubric suggests six areas you can evaluate to determine your competence and effectiveness as an intercultural communicator. Evaluate yourself in these six areas:

Knowledge Area #1: Knowledge of your own culture

0	1	2	3	4
(Deficient)	(Basic)	(Intermediate)	(Advanced)	(Expert)

Knowledge Area #2: Knowledge of other cultures

0	1	2	3	4
(Deficient)	(Basic)	(Intermediate)	(Advanced)	(Expert)

Skill Area #1: Empathy

0	1	2	3	4
(Deficient)	(Basic)	(Intermediate)	(Advanced)	(Expert)

Skill Area #2: Verbal/Nonverbal Communication

0	1	2	3	4
(Deficient)	(Basic)	(Intermediate)	(Advanced)	(Expert)

Attitude Area #1: Curiosity

0	1	2	3	4
(Deficient)	(Basic)	(Intermediate)	(Advanced)	(Expert)

Attitude Area #2: Openness

0	1	2	3	4
(Deficient)	(Basic)	(Intermediate)	(Advanced)	(Expert)

What are your strongest areas as an intercultural communicator? Why do you think you are strong in these areas?

_____

_____

_____

_____

_____

What are your weakest areas as an intercultural communicator? Why do you think you are weak in these areas?

_____

_____

_____

_____

_____

Knowing your strengths and weaknesses as an intercultural communicator, what can you do to increase your intercultural communication competence?

_____

_____

_____

_____

_____

The first three sub-areas of the IES by The Kozai Group (self-awareness, exploration, and global mindset) will be strengthened by using the textbook and this workbook. However, the second three sub-areas (relationship interest, positive regard, and emotional resilience) will primarily be strengthened by having intercultural interactions.

How can you increase the quantity and quality of your intercultural interactions?

_____

_____

_____

_____

_____

Name: _____   Period: _____

ICC Chapter 1 Quiz

Match each term with its corresponding definition.

1. Culture _____   2. Co-culture _____   3. Deep-structure institutions ___

4. Acculturation _____   5. Enculturation _____   6. Cultural artifacts _____

7. Dominant culture _____   8. Popular culture _____   9. National culture _____

   A. A process in which members of one culture adopt the beliefs, values, or behaviors of another cultural group.
   B. An interdependent but equal cultural group that exists in a dominant or national culture.
   C. Objects made by human beings that give information about a culture.
   D. Learned beliefs, values, attitudes, and behaviors that bind a group of people together.
   E. The social organizations of family, church, and state that have created, transmitted, maintained, and reinforced the basic elements of every traditional culture.
   F. The culture created by those who have the greatest influence on the beliefs, values, and customs of a people group. (Also called *umbrella culture* or *mainstream culture*)
   G. The process whereby people learn their group's culture through observation and instruction. This process begins at a very early age.
   H. Cultural products and artifacts that are widely disseminated and consumed.
   I. The common beliefs, values, and behaviors that exist within the population of a sovereign nation.

10. Globalization _____   11. Cosmopolitanism _____   12. Intercultural communication __

13. Openness _____   14. Empathy _____   15. Emotional resilience _____

16. Communication _____   17. Curiosity _____   18. Positive regard _____

   A. The process of sending and receiving messages through verbal or nonverbal symbols.
   B. Communication between people from substantially different cultural groups.
   C. The idea that all human beings are citizens in a single world community.
   D. The tendency toward worldwide integration of economic and communication systems.
   E. The desire to learn and know more about something or someone.
   F. The ability to understand and relate to the thoughts and feelings of others.
   G. Receptiveness to new or different ideas, experiences, and people.
   H. Basic acceptance, support, and respect of other people.
   I. The ability to cope with stress and adversity.

19. T. or F.   There are approximately 300 national cultures in the world.

20. T. or F.   Whereas people usually belong to only one national culture, they may belong to dozens of co-cultures.

21. T. or F.   The term "subculture" is now more acceptable than the term "co-culture."

22. T. or F.   The social group that primarily transmits cultural beliefs, values, and behaviors is the family.

23. T. or F.   The ethnic group with the greatest numerical advantage creates the dominant national culture of a country.

24. T. or F.   Human culture would not exist without communication, and human communication would not exist without culture.

25. T. or F.   Culture is an important concept and field of study in six different academic areas.

26. Which of the following is a primary function of culture?
    A. Culture gives meaning to events and actions.
    B. Culture gives people their identities.
    C. Culture provides people with a pattern for living and teaches people how to adapt to their surroundings.
    D. All of the above.

27. Which of the following similes of culture emphasizes that culture influences your perceptions?
    A. Culture is like a fishbowl.
    B. Culture is like a pair of glasses.
    C. Culture is like a computer operating system.
    D. Culture is like an iceberg.

28. Using the iceberg simile, which element of culture is "above the surface" and observable?
    A. beliefs   B. values   C. attitudes   D. behaviors

29. Which of the following is an important characteristic of culture?
    A. Culture is passed from one generation to the next.
    B. Culture is dynamic.
    C. Culture is an integrated system.
    D. All of the above.

30. Most scholars trace the beginning of the study of Intercultural Communication to anthropologist
_____ who first used the term
"intercultural communication" in his 1959 book, *The Silent Language*.

Name: _____   Period: _____

ICC Chapter 1 Activity Sheet #1

Co-Culture Report Sheet

If this handwritten co-culture report sheet is filled out completely, it should translate into a five-minute oral report or a one-page typed, single-spaced, written report. To practice being a cultural ambassador, report out on a co-culture to which you belong (or have belonged).

Co-culture: _____

_____

Relationship to Dominant American Culture: _____

_____

_____

Values and Beliefs: _____

_____

_____

_____

_____

_____

_____

Distinctive Material Possessions, Clothing, and/or Grooming: _____

_____

_____

_____

_____

_____

_____

_____

Behaviors, Rituals, and Activities: _____

_____

_____

_____

_____

_____

Language, Slang, Expressions Used by Co-Culture: _____

_____

_____

_____

_____

Misunderstandings or Incorrect Assumptions About Co-Culture: _____

_____

_____

_____

Elements of Co-Culture To Be Appreciated: _____

_____

_____

_____

Name: _____   Period: _____

ICC Chapter 1 Activity Sheet #2

National Culture Report Sheet

If this hand-written national culture report sheet is filled out completely, it should translate into a 10-minute oral report or a two-page typed, single-spaced written report. If you report out on a national culture, avoid ethnocentric evaluations or statements. Show respect for the national culture and demonstrate positive regard for the people who live in that country.

COUNTRY: _____

NATIVE OR OFFICIAL NAME: _____

IMPORTANCE OR CONNECTION TO U.S.: _____

_____

_____

CONTINENT: _____

BORDERING COUNTRIES: _____

_____

_____

AREA: _____ AREA RANK: _____

POPULATION: _____ RANK: _____

CAPITAL: _____

FLAG AND OTHER NATIONAL SYMBOLS: _____

_____

_____

_____

NATIONAL VALUES: _____

_____

_____

_____

TYPE OF GOVERNMENT: _____

_____

_____

GEOGRAPHY AND CLIMATE: _____

_____

_____

_____

_____

_____

_____

HISTORY (FOCUSING ON PEOPLE GROUPS IN COUNTRY): _____

_____

_____

_____

_____

_____

_____

_____

_____

_____

_____

ETHNIC GROUPS: _____

_____

_____

LANGUAGES: _____

_____

_____

RELIGIONS: _____

_____

_____

FOOD AND DRINK: _____

_____

_____

_____

DINING ETIQUETTE: _____

_____

_____

_____

CLOTHING/FASHION: _____

_____

_____

_____

MUSIC: _____

_____

_____

_____

ART: _____

_____

_____

_____

SPORTS: _____

_____

_____

_____

LEISURE ACTIVITIES: _____

_____

_____

_____

COMMON WORDS AND PHRASES: _____

_____

_____

_____

COMMUNICATION TIPS: _____

_____

_____

_____

MOVIES, TV SHOWS, BOOKS, WEBSITES FROM THE COUNTRY: _____

_____

_____

_____

_____

Chapter Evaluation   Name: _____
Chapter: _____   Class: _____

Most difficult or confusing ideas from the chapter:

1. _____

_____

_____

2. _____

_____

_____

Most controversial or hard to accept ideas from the chapter:

1. _____

_____

_____

2. _____

_____

_____

Suggestions for improving the chapter:

1. _____

_____

_____

2. _____

_____

_____

Most important or useful ideas from the chapter:

1. _____

_____

_____

2. _____

_____

_____

3. _____

_____

_____

Most important chapter skills and/or attitudes to develop:

1. _____

_____

_____

2. _____

_____

_____

Questions generated by reading the chapter:

1. _____

_____

_____

2. _____

_____

_____

Chapter 2

Appreciating Both Sameness and Difference

Chapter Learning Objectives

(Check off when you think the learning objective has been achieved.)

1. _____ Recognize two contrasting approaches for dealing with people and cultures: focusing on sameness and focusing on difference.

2. _____ Understand the role that cognitive restructuring can play in developing intercultural communication competence.

3. _____ Learn to appreciate sameness and difference by understanding the positive consequences of both and the negative consequences of over-emphasizing either.

4. _____ Learn to balance between contrasting and complementary concepts or values.

5. _____ Understand and explain the difference between valid generalizations and invalid stereotypes.

6. _____ Develop an awareness of the negative effects of stereotypes, ethnocentrism, prejudice, and discrimination.

7. _____ Recognize the symptoms and stages of culture shock, and develop the capacity to adjust to new and different cultural experiences.

Workbook Handouts

(Check off when each handout has been completed.)

_____ Chapter 2 Reading Guide (6 pages)

_____ Chapter 2 Journal #1 (Sameness and Difference Part 1) (2 pages)

_____ Chapter 2 Journal #2 (Sameness and Difference Part 2) (2 pages)

_____ Chapter 2 Quiz (2 pages)

_____ Chapter 2 Activity Sheet #1 (Generalizations and Stereotypes) (2 pages)

_____ Chapter 2 Activity Sheet #2 (Sensitivity Training) (2 pages)

_____ Chapter 2 Activity Sheet #3 (National Culture Distinctives) (2 pages)

_____ Chapter 2 Evaluation (2 pages)

Name: _____   Period: _____

ICC Chapter 2 Reading Guide

Why was the Universal Declaration of Human Rights (UDHR) adopted by the United Nations General Assembly?

_____

_____

_____

What does the Universal Declaration of Human Rightsespouse AND assert?

_____

_____

What does The Developmental Model of Intercultural Sensitivity (DMIS) provide?

_____

_____

List Milton Bennett's six stages of intercultural sensitivity:

1. _____

2. _____

3. _____

4. _____

5. _____

6. _____

According to the textbook, which approach, the Universal Declaration of Human Rights or the Developmental Model of Intercultural Sensitivity, is best? Explain why.

_____

_____

_____

Define what cognitive restructuring is, AND explain how it applies to the "iceberg simile" from Chapter 1.

_____

_____

_____

_____

Explain how cognitive restructuring needs to occur in intercultural interactions and intercultural communication:

_____

_____

_____

List AND define the five reasons to **appreciate sameness**:

1. _____

   _____

2. _____

   _____

3. _____

   _____

4. _____

   _____

5. _____

   _____

List AND define the five reasons to **appreciate difference**:

1. _____

   _____

2. _____

   _____

3. _____

_____

4. _____

_____

5. _____

List AND explain the five problems related to **privileging sameness**:

1. _____

_____

2. _____

_____

3. _____

_____

4. _____

_____

5. _____

_____

Explain two major differences that distinguish valid generalizations from invalid stereotypes:

_____

_____

_____

_____

_____

_____

What is "embodied ethnocentrism?" Should you seek to completely eliminate it?

_____

_____

_____

Define the term "xenophobia":

_____

_____

What is "colorblindness," and how does it create problems?

_____

_____

_____

_____

List and explain the five problems related to **privileging difference**:

1. _____

_____

2. _____

_____

3. _____

_____

4. _____

_____

5. _____

_____

What are the four stages of the U-Curve Theory?

1. _____

_____

2. _____

_____

3. _____

_____

4. _____

_____

Define the phrase "reverse culture shock" :

_____

_____

_____

List three ways someone might reduce culture shock:

1. _____

2. _____

3. _____

What is "scientific racism," and when was it discredited?

_____

_____

_____

_____

Explain the sameness/difference bias of Eastern cultures and Western cultures:

_____

_____

_____

_____

What can you do if you discover in yourself a bias toward either sameness or difference?

_____

_____

_____

According to the textbook, what example do we have from the East of the balance between contrasting concepts or values? Briefly describe this Eastern concept or philosophical principle.

_____

_____

_____

List and describe the five examples from the West of the balance between contrasting concepts or values:

1. _____

_____

2. _____

_____

3. _____

_____

4. _____

_____

5. _____

_____

Name: _____   Period: _____

ICC Chapter 2 Journal #1

Sameness and Difference Part 1

Compare your Chapter 2 Post-Test to your Chapter 2 Pre-Test. Did your "x" move on the sameness/difference continuum line? If it did not, why not? If it did, why?

_____

_____

_____

_____

_____

After reading Chapter 2, do you think you have developed an appreciation for both sameness and difference? Explain your answer.

_____

_____

_____

_____

_____

Do you think the Universal Declaration of Human rights is a valid document? Why or why not?

_____

_____

_____

_____

Do you lean more toward moral universalism or moral relativism? Explain your answer.

_____

_____

_____

_____

_____

Which cultural patterns in the "patterns and pattern recognition" section of Chapter 2 do you find most important or useful? Why?

_____

_____

_____

_____

_____

Relate one specific example of a time when you were a victim of prejudice, ethnocentrism, stereotyping, or discrimination:

_____

_____

_____

_____

_____

_____

Relate one specific example of a time when you were a perpetrator of prejudice, ethnocentrism, stereotyping, or discrimination:

_____

_____

_____

_____

_____

Name: _____   Period: _____

ICC Chapter 2 Journal #2

Sameness and Difference Part 2

After reading the Rudyard Kipling poem "We and They," identify the ethnocentric words or phrases in this poem. What words or phrases indicate that people are making negative value judgments just because others are different from themselves?

_____

_____

_____

_____

_____

Do you think people should strive to eradicate all ethnocentrism in themselves? Explain your answer.

_____

_____

_____

_____

_____

Why is it problematic to ignore whether a person is male or female?

_____

_____

_____

_____

Why is it problematic to ignore the color of a person's skin? What is wrong with the "colorblind" approach to race relations?

_____

_____

_____

_____

Describe in detail one time when you or someone you know experienced culture shock:

_____

_____

_____

_____

_____

Are your important interpersonal relationships primarily based upon the similarity principle or the complementarity principle? Explain your answer.

_____

_____

_____

_____

_____

_____

Are you wired primarily for stability and predictability or for variety and novelty? Explain.

_____

_____

_____

_____

_____

Do you prefer the "melting pot" metaphor or the "salad bowl" metaphor for America? Why?

_____

_____

_____

_____

_____

Name: _____   Period: _____

ICC Chapter 2 Quiz

Match each term with its corresponding definition.

1. Homogeneous _____   2. Heterogeneous _____   3. Monoculturalism _____

4. Multiculturalism _____   5. Stability _____   6. Variety _____

7. Dialectical tensions _____   8. Pattern _____

9. Similarity principle _____   10. Complementarity principle _____

11. Moral universalism _____   12. Moral relativism _____

   A. Interpersonal attraction based on the differences between people.
   B. Opposing forces that people experience in their relationships; the tension between two desirable goals or values.
   C. The quality or state of something that is not easily changed.
   D. Interpersonal attraction based on the similarities between people.
   E. Composed of different parts or people.
   F. Made up of the same kind of people or things.
   G. Something that repeats in a predictable, intelligible way; an arrangement or sequence regularly found in objects or events.
   H. An ethical philosophy that emphasizes difference and argues that different cultures and individuals have different standards of right and wrong.
   I. An ethical philosophy that emphasizes sameness and argues that certain human behaviors are right or wrong regardless of circumstances.
   J. The practice of actively preserving a national culture by excluding external cultural influences.
   K. The idea that several different co-cultures can coexist peacefully and equally in one national culture.
   L. The quality or state of being different or diverse.

13. Recalibration _____   14. National character _____   15. Culture shock _____

16. U-Curve theory _____   17. Generalization _____   18. Stereotype _____

19. Prejudice _____   20. Ethnocentrism _____   21. Xenophobia _____

22. Othering _____   23. Colorblindness _____   24. Discrimination _____

   A. Extreme fear or hatred of strangers or foreigners.
   B. Not recognizing skin color or racial distinctions.
   C. A theory in intercultural studies that describes culture shock, adjustment, and acculturation as stages in a process.
   D. The disorientation and confusion a person experiences when suddenly exposed to a different culture or society.

E. An invalid generalization applied universally to an entire group with insufficient evidence.

F. Unfair treatment of people, often motivated by prejudice; (alternate definition) the ability to see or make fine distinctions.

G. The belief in the inherent superiority of one's own ethnic group or culture.

H. A statement or assertion applied to a large group of people or things.

I. Making mental adjustments and transforming your thinking so you appreciate people because of your differences rather than in spite of your differences.

J. An unfavorable and unjustified feeling of dislike, disdain, or hatred for a person or group of people because of race, sex, religion, age, etc.

K. A mental activity whereby an individual or group is classified as different, alien, and "not one of us."

L. A group of characteristics or behavioral traits that apply to the majority population of a whole nation.

25. T. or F.   The U.N. Universal Declaration of Human rights focuses on difference, whereas the Bennett Scale focuses on sameness.

26. T. or F.   Merely recognizing similarities and differences between people and cultures is not good enough: you need to recognize and appreciate both sameness and difference.

27. A psychological process that can help people change their attitudes and behaviors is called

_____ _____.

28. T. or F.   To become an effective intercultural communicator, you do not need to abandon or replace the core beliefs and values of your home culture.

29. T. or F.   Religious beliefs just cause divisions among people.

30. T. or F.   The term "discrimination" has no positive meaning.

31. T. or F.   You should avoid making generalizations about other people.

32. T. or F.   Stereotypes are okay as long as they are positive stereotypes.

33. T. or F.   Embodied ethnocentrism is an extreme form of ethnocentrism to be eliminated.

34. T. or F.   A good approach to race relations is the concept of "colorblindness."

35. People who are suddenly thrust into a very different culture can experience

_____ _____.

Name: _____   Period: _____

ICC Chapter 2 Activity Sheet #1

Generalizations and Stereotypes

As Figure 2.18 of Chapter 2 reveals, stereotypes are at the heart of many bad attitudes and behaviors. Stereotypes are invalid generalizations, untrue beliefs, that often lead to ethnocentrism, prejudice, and discrimination. You should avoid stereotyping, and you should discourage others from stereotyping.

However, human beings could not think or communicate without making valid generalizations. In order to make sense of our world, we must generalize and place things in categories.

Identify whether the following statements or assertions are based on valid generalizations or invalid stereotypes. (Remember, valid generalizations are preceded by "qualifier words" and are not assumed without evidence.)

1. "Generally, many women are more emotionally expressive than many men."

    (Valid generalization/Invalid stereotype) Explanation: _____

    _____

2. "Males are more logical than females."

    (Valid generalization/Invalid stereotype) Explanation: _____

    _____

3. "Since Mark is a man, he must be insensitive." _____

    (Valid generalization/Invalid stereotype) Explanation: _____

    _____

4. "Since Phyllis is a woman, she may have a tendency to use powerless language." _____

    (Valid generalization/Invalid stereotype) Explanation: _____

    _____

5. "Mexicans prefer to marry young." _____

    (Valid generalization/Invalid stereotype) Explanation: _____

    _____

6. "No American wants to see communism flourish." _____

    (Valid generalization/Invalid stereotype) Explanation: _____

    _____

7. "Since Kwan is Asian, he wants his children to go to college."_____

    (Valid generalization/Invalid stereotype) Explanation:_____

    _____

8. "Since John is a black American, there is a good chance he has experienced acts of discrimination."

    (Valid generalization/Invalid stereotype) Explanation: _____

    _____

9. "The majority of white Americans are unaware of their white privilege and preferential treatment."

    (Valid generalization/Invalid stereotype) Explanation:_____

    _____

10. "Japanese citizens are hard-working, industrious people."_____

    (Valid generalization/Invalid stereotype) Explanation:_____

    _____

Write out what you consider to be two valid generalizations:

Valid generalization #1: _____

_____

Valid generalization #2: _____

_____

Write out a common stereotype: _____

_____

Explain why this stereotype is harmful or offensive: _____

_____

_____

Name: _____   Period: _____

ICC Chapter 2 Activity Sheet #2

Sensitivity Training

Identify which people groups you are most likely to have prejudices toward:

People Group	Amount of Prejudice of Which You are Consciously Aware					
	none	very little	some	fair amount	high amount	extreme
	0	**1**	**2**	**3**	**4**	**5**
Children:	0	1	2	3	4	5
Old people:	0	1	2	3	4	5
Men:	0	1	2	3	4	5
Women:	0	1	2	3	4	5
Poor people:	0	1	2	3	4	5
Middle-class people:	0	1	2	3	4	5
Rich people:	0	1	2	3	4	5
Blue-collar workers:	0	1	2	3	4	5
White-collar workers:	0	1	2	3	4	5
Gradeschool-educated:	0	1	2	3	4	5
College-educated people:	0	1	2	3	4	5
Caucasians/Whites:	0	1	2	3	4	5
African-Americans/Blacks:	0	1	2	3	4	5
Asians:	0	1	2	3	4	5
Hispanics:	0	1	2	3	4	5
Native Americans:	0	1	2	3	4	5
Heterosexuals:	0	1	2	3	4	5
Homosexuals:	0	1	2	3	4	5
Celibates:	0	1	2	3	4	5

People Group	Amount of Prejudice of which You Are Consciously Aware					
	none	very little	some	fair amount	high amount	extreme
	0	**1**	**2**	**3**	**4**	**5**
Atheists:	0	1	2	3	4	5
Agnostics/Non-religious people:	0	1	2	3	4	5
Devout religious believers:	0	1	2	3	4	5
Jews:	0	1	2	3	4	5
Christians:	0	1	2	3	4	5
Muslims:	0	1	2	3	4	5
Hindus:	0	1	2	3	4	5
Buddhists:	0	1	2	3	4	5
Sikhs:	0	1	2	3	4	5

If you identified a fair/high/extreme amount of conscious prejudice for any people group, why do you think you might have this prejudice? What has created this prejudice in you?

_____

_____

_____

_____

_____

_____

Toward which people groups do you suspect you might have unconscious prejudice? Why?

_____

_____

_____

_____

Name: _____   Period: _____

ICC Chapter 2 Activity Sheet #3

National Culture Distinctives

To develop an appreciation for different national cultures and for some of the elements that make them distinctive or unique, match the following dances, alcoholic beverages, and foods with the appropriate country.

DANCE	**ALCOHOLIC BEVERAGE**	**FOOD**
1. Bambuca _____	1. Baijiu _____	1. Borscht _____
2. Belly dance _____	2. Beer _____	2. Caviar _____
3. Dragon dance _____	3. Cachaca _____	3. Ceviche _____
4. Flamenco _____	4. Palinka _____	4. Chow mein _____
5. Hat dance _____	5. Rum _____	5. Fish and chips _____
6. Hip hop _____	6. Sake _____	6. Kimchi _____
7. Polka _____	7. Scotch _____	7. Mole _____
8. Samba _____	8. Tequila _____	8. Paella _____
9. Tango _____	9. Vodka _____	9. Souffle _____
10. Waltz _____	10. Wine _____	10. Sushi _____

COUNTRY	**COUNTRY**	**COUNTRY**
A. Austria	A. Brazil	A. China
B. Argentina	B. China	B. France
C. Brazil	C. France	C. Japan
D. China	D. Germany	D. Korea
E. Colombia	E. Hungary	E. Mexico
F. Czech Republic	F. Jamaica	F. Peru
G. Egypt	G. Japan	G. Russia
H. Mexico	H. Mexico	H. Spain
I. Spain	I. Russia	I. Ukraine
J. United States	J. Scotland	J. United Kingdom

Answers to National Culture Distinctives

DANCE

1. Bambuca: E. Colombia
2. Belly dance: G. Egypt
3. Dragon dance: D. China
4. Flamenco: I. Spain
5. Hat dance: H. Mexico
6. Hip hop: J. US
7. Polka: F. Czech Republic
8. Samba: C. Brazil
9. Tango: B. Argentina
10. Waltz: A. Austria

ALCOHOLIC BEVERAGE

1. Baijiu: B. China
2. Beer: D. Germany
3. Cachaca: A. Brazil
4. Palinka: E. Hungary
5. Rum: F. Jamaica
6. Sake: G. Japan
7. Scotch: J. Scotland
8. Tequila: H. Mexico
9. Vodka: I. Russia
10. Wine: C. France

FOOD

1. Borscht: I. Ukraine
2. Caviar: G. Russia
3. Ceviche: F. Peru
4. Chow mein: A. China
5. Fish and chips: J. United Kingdom
6. Kimchi: D. Korea
7. Mole: E. Mexico
8. Paella: H. Spain
9. Souffle: B. France
10. Sushi: C. Japan

Chapter Evaluation

Name: _____

Chapter: _____

Class: _____

Most difficult or confusing ideas from the chapter:

1. _____

   _____

   _____

2. _____

   _____

   _____

Most controversial or hard to accept ideas from the chapter:

1. _____

   _____

   _____

2. _____

   _____

   _____

Suggestions for improving the chapter:

1. _____

   _____

   _____

2. _____

   _____

   _____

Most important or useful ideas from the chapter:

1. _____

   _____

   _____

2. _____

   _____

   _____

3. _____

   _____

   _____

Most important chapter skills and/or attitudes to develop:

1. _____

   _____

   _____

2. _____

   _____

   _____

Questions generated by reading the chapter:

1. _____

   _____

   _____

2. _____

   _____

   _____

Chapter 3

Adaptation and Empathy

Chapter Learning Objectives

(Check off when you think a learning objective has been achieved.)

1. _____ Gain an understanding of historical perspectives regarding adaptation.

2. _____ Identify and explain the Bennett Scale for cultural adaptation.

3. _____ Develop skill in the use of empathy across a variety of situations.

Workbook Handouts

(Check off when each handout has been completed.)

_____ Chapter 3 Reading Guide (6 pages)

_____ Chapter 3 Journal #1 (4 pages)

_____ Chapter 3 Quiz (2 pages)

_____ Chapter 3 Activity Sheet #1 (The Bennett Scale and Acting With Empathy) (2 pages)

_____ Chapter 3 Evaluation (2 pages)

Name: _____   Period: _____

Chapter 3 Reading Guide

What is meant by the cliché "When in Rome, do as the Romans do"?

_____

_____

Explain what the "melting pot" metaphor is:

_____

_____

According to the text, what do integration and desegregation refer to?

_____

_____

Why did Milton Bennett create the Developmental Model of Intercultural Sensitivity?

_____

_____

Provide three reasons that Bennett's scale is helpful:

1. _____

_____

2. _____

_____

3. _____

_____

What warning is provided when using The Bennett Scale?

_____

_____

_____

Define the term "denial":

_____

_____

Provide two ways to grow beyond the denial of difference:

1. _____

_____

2. _____

_____

Explain what the "defense" stage is:

_____

_____

Provide two ways to grow beyond defensiveness:

1. _____

_____

2. _____

_____

Give two reasons why it is dangerous to focus only on similarities:

1. _____

_____

2. _____

_____

Describe the "minimization" stage AND what it can result in:

_____

_____

_____

_____

Provide two ways to grow beyond minimization of difference:

1. _____

   _____

2. _____

   _____

Describe the "acceptance" stage of difference:

_____

_____

Define the following terms in reference to growing beyond acceptance of difference:

Cultural relativists: _____

_____

Ethnorelativists: _____

_____

Social justice advocates: _____

_____

Describe what characterizes the "adaptation" stage: _____

_____

_____

Provide three ways to grow beyond adaptation to difference:

1. _____

   _____

2. _____

_____

3. _____

_____

When we reach the integration stage, how do we tend to see ourselves?

_____

_____

Provide two ways to grow beyond the "integration" stage:

1. _____

_____

2. _____

_____

Define the term "empathy" when we refer to it in intercultural communication:

_____

_____

List AND define the two types of empathy described by the Greater Good Science Society, University of California, Berkeley:

1. _____

_____

2. _____

_____

Provide three ways to increase your empathy skills:

1. _____

2. _____

3. _____

Give six tips to help find in-the-moment mindfulness:

1. _____

2. _____

3. _____

4. _____

5. _____

6. _____

Define the phrase "emotional intelligence":

_____

_____

Provide three tips to help increase your emotional intelligence:

1. _____

2. _____

3. _____

According to the text, why does empathy leave us? _____

_____

List the six ways to build empathy through perspective taking suggested by the textbook:

1. _____

2. _____

3. _____

4. _____

5. _____

6. _____

Describe how you can build empathy by regulating your own emotional responses:

_____

_____

Define what "The Platinum Rule" is:

_____

_____

Explain how "Ting" helps us to listen with empathy:

_____

_____

How do defensive and non-defensive communication skills differ?

_____

_____

_____

List the five elements of emotional resilience

1. _____   4. _____

2. _____   5. _____

3. _____

Provide the four methods to jumpstart the cycle of positive regard:

1. _____

2. _____

3. _____

_____

4. _____

_____

Name: _____ Period: _____

ICC Chapter 3 Journal #1

What do you think of the advice "When in Rome, do as the Romans do." Explain your answer.

_____

_____

_____

_____

Circle the developmental stage of the Bennett Scale you think you are currently in:

Denial   Defense   Minimization   Acceptance   Adaptation   Integration

Explain why you think you are in this developmental stage. Give specific examples.

_____

_____

_____

_____

_____

_____

_____

_____

What developmental stage, realistically, do you think you will be in at the end of this semester? Explain your answer.

_____

_____

_____

_____

_____

_____

The textbook points out that cognitive empathy is the ability to imagine what someone is thinking or feeling. How well-developed is your cognitive empathy ability? Explain your answer.

_____

_____

_____

_____

_____

How often do you practice "in-the-moment mindfulness?" ? Explain your answer.

_____

_____

_____

_____

Would you like to increase your in-the-moment mindfulness? Why or why not?

_____

_____

_____

_____

What is your emotional intelligence quotient? How much emotional intelligence do you have? Explain your answer.

_____

_____

_____

_____

_____

When you forget to empathize, what typically gets in the way of your empathy response?

_____

_____

_____

_____

_____

Can you see yourself using Dr. John Medina's "empathy reflex" technique? Why or why not?

_____

_____

_____

_____

_____

How often do you read literary fiction? Do you think reading literary fiction improves a person's ability to empathize? Explain your answer.

_____

_____

_____

_____

_____

Do you think it is possible to accept and support others even when you disagree with their choices or behaviors? Explain your answer.

_____

_____

_____

_____

_____

_____

Do you think "The Platinum Rule" is better or more useful than "The Golden Rule"? Why or why not?

_____

_____

_____

_____

What do you think of Balpreet Kaur's nondefensive communication skills?

_____

_____

_____

_____

How emotionally resilient are you? Why do you think this is the case?

_____

_____

_____

_____

_____

Do you find it easy or difficult to have positive regard for others? Explain your answer.

_____

_____

_____

_____

Name: _____   Period: _____

ICC Chapter 3 Quiz

Match the terms with their appropriate definitions.

1. Acceptance _____   2. Adaptation _____   3. Defense _____

4. Denial _____   5. Minimization _____   6. Integration _____

7. Ethnocentric response _____   8. Ethnorelative response _____

   A. The first step of the Bennett model: an ethnocentric response in which we ignore differences, and when confronted by differences, we are either confused, unsettled, or wholly blind to them.
   B. The second step of the Bennett model: an ethnocentric response in which we become protective of our own experiences and devalue experiences that are not like our own.
   C. The third step of the Bennett model: an ethnocentric response in which we focus solely on the similarities between ourselves and others.
   D. The fourth step of the Bennett model: an ethnorelative response in which we accept both the similarities and differences in others.
   E. The fifth step of the Bennett model: an ethnorelative response in which we learn to empathize, to shift frames of reference, and to enact our intercultural communication skills.
   F. The sixth step of the Bennett model: an ethnorelative response in which we develop a marginal identity, an identity that includes behaviors and beliefs of both the home and the host culture.
   G. When communicators rely on experiences of both their home and host cultures to interpret new experiences and make behavioral choices.
   H. When communicators rely solely on their own experiences of their own culture to interpret new experiences and make behavioral choices.

9. Affective empathy _____   10. Cognitive empathy _____   11. Ting _____

12. Empathy reflex _____   13. Perspective taking _____   14. Social coping _____

15. Emotional hardiness _____   16. Emotional intelligence _____   17. Platinum rule _____

18. Positive regard _____   19. Emotional resilience _____

20. Meaning-focused coping _____

   A. The Chinese character meaning "to listen." The character includes listening with your ears, eyes, full attention, and heart.
   B. Relying on social connections that provide support in trying times, bolster our sense of self, and help us to remain resilient in trying times.
   C. Do to others as they would have done to them.
   D. When we treat others as though their motives are pure.
   E. When we find ourselves in difficult situations and we focus not on how hard things are, but, instead, on what we will learn from the experience.
   F. Our ability to bounce back after we've experienced stress.
   G. The ability to recognize our own emotions, discern what our emotions are trying to tell us, and understand the impact our behaviors related to our emotional states have on others.

H. A term used to describe people who deal well with stressful situations.

I. Rather than mirroring volatile emotions and reacting with equal force, describing instead the emotions you are seeing and making a guess as to the cause of all of the emotions.

J. The emotional response we feel when we witness someone experiencing emotions.

K. The ability to imagine what someone is thinking or feeling.

L. Actively imagining what another person is experiencing. Considering the other person's experiences, difficulties, beliefs, values, and rules for behavior.

21. The Melting Pot Metaphor is an example of cultural _____.

22. T. or F.   In order to connect more fully with the experiences of others, we need to learn to question our own viewpoints and become open to perspectives that differ from our own.

23. T. or F.   If you work hard over a short period of time, you should be able to progress through all six stages of the Bennett Scale.

24. T. or F.   Defense, Denial, and Minimization are the ethnorelative stages of the Bennett Scale, whereas Acceptance, Adaptation, and Integration are the ethnocentric stages.

25. T. or F.   In intercultural communication, empathy is simply being able to mirror the feelings of others.

26. Cognitive empathy is often referred to as _____

_____ .

27. T. or F.   People who act with empathy in their marriages often feel greater intimacy and satisfaction in their relationships.

28. T. or F.   Doctors who show empathy have healthier patients but enjoy worse health themselves.

29. T. or F.   To develop in-the-moment-mindfulness, you should savor great moments.

30. T. or F.   Empathy leaves us when we are focused on ourselves and our own needs or interests.

31. T. or F.   Readers of fiction tend to show less empathy for others.

32. T. or F.   People who have had Botox treatments have more difficulty empathizing with others.

33. T. or F.   Validating and accepting the experience of others can help you maintain a personal connection with them.

34. T. or F.   The Platinum Rule says, "Do to others as you would have them do to you."

35. _____ allows us to survive, and sometimes thrive, in difficult situations.

Name: _____   Period: _____

ICC Chapter 3 Activity Sheet #1

Activity: The Bennett Scale

Dante grew up in San Gabriel, California. After college he was hired at a firm in downtown Los Angeles, just 10 miles from San Gabriel. As a result of his exceptional sales, he got a promotion at work that included a move to Toronto, Ontario, Canada. After 2 months in Canada, Dante has noticed that his laid-back style, a key to his promotion, isn't always appreciated by his peers at work. Here's a note he sent to a friend regarding his frustration:

"It looks just like home but there's this crazy summer humidity that makes me wish for just one cool Pacific breeze. The people here are a little different too. At first, I thought they were just like everyone at home, but then I noticed they were way more standoffish. They don't seem to like me. . .I don't get it. Everybody likes me! They're getting under my skin. I can't seem to do anything right. I'm not sure I'm gonna make it here."

Look back at the section of the chapter titled, "Learning to Adapt." Look through the discussion of the Bennett Scale to answer the following questions:

1) Which part of the Bennett Scale is Dante currently experiencing?

_____

2) What word choices indicate to you that he is experiencing the above part of the Bennett Scale?

_____

_____

3) What level of the Bennett scale do you think Dante will have to reach in order to become as successful as he was in Los Angeles?

_____

4) Why do you think it will be necessary for him to reach that level of the Bennett scale in order to regain his success?

_____

_____

_____

5) Based on your reading, what advice would you give Dante to help him adapt and thrive in his current situation?

_____

_____

_____

_____

Activity: Acting with Empathy

Imagine that you have a fun evening planned with a friend. You've been looking forward to this for weeks, and after your especially difficult week, you need to blow off steam. You arrive at the agreed upon time, but, as you look around, your friend is nowhere to be found. You text her and you receive no immediate reply. Several minutes later, she texts back, "Running late. . .Be there as soon as I can." Over an hour later she arrives, flustered and smiling. By then you've just about had it, and you are ready to go home. You are disappointed and annoyed.

Based on your reading regarding empathy, what are five different ways you can salvage this night and maintain your friendship (there are more than five but just list five)? *Hint: The advice is not in one single list, but is, instead, found throughout the last half of the chapter.*

1) _____

_____

_____

_____

2) _____

_____

_____

_____

3) _____

_____

_____

_____

4) _____

_____

_____

_____

5) _____

_____

Chapter Evaluation

Chapter: _____

Name: _____

Class: _____

Most difficult or confusing ideas from the chapter:

1. _____

_____

_____

2. _____

_____

_____

Most controversial or hard to accept ideas from the chapter:

1. _____

_____

_____

2. _____

_____

_____

Suggestions for improving the chapter:

1. _____

_____

_____

2. _____

_____

_____

Most important or useful ideas from the chapter:

1. _____

_____

_____

2. _____

_____

_____

3. _____

_____

_____

Most important chapter skills and/or attitudes to develop:

1. _____

_____

_____

2. _____

_____

_____

Questions generated by reading the chapter:

1. _____

_____

_____

2. _____

_____

_____

Chapter 4

Verbal Communication

Chapter Learning Objectives

(Check off when you think a learning objective has been achieved.)

1. _____ Identify the levels of language.

2. _____ Learn about the many languages on our planet.

3. _____ Gain an awareness of the ways linguistic relativity shapes our perceptions.

4. _____ Learn ways to avoid misunderstandings and what to do when we offend.

Workbook Handouts

(Check off when each handout has been completed.)

_____ Chapter 4 Reading Guide (4 pages)

_____ Chapter 4 Journal #1 (4 pages)

_____ Chapter 4 Quiz (2 pages)

_____ Chapter 4 Activity Sheet #1 (Linguistic Differences and Linguistic Relativity) (2 pages)

_____ Chapter 4 Activity Sheet #2 (Blame Placing and High/Low Context Styles) (2 pages)

_____ Chapter 4 Evaluation (2 pages)

Name: _____   Period: _____

ICC Chapter 4 Reading Guide

Verbal Communication

List AND define the four levels of language that exist across the languages of the earth:

1. _____

_____

2. _____

_____

3. _____

_____

4. _____

_____

Explain what tonal languages are:

_____

_____

What is the difference between a <u>language family</u> and an <u>isolate</u>?

_____

_____

Explain what a **translator** does: _____

_____

_____

_____

Describe what the best **interpreters** do: _____

_____

_____

Explain the Sapir-Whorf hypothesis: _____

_____

_____

List AND provide an example of the three ways language influences us:

1. _____

   _____

2. _____

   _____

3. _____

   _____

Explain the difference between low context and high context communication:

_____

_____

_____

_____

Provide an example of a high context communication culture: _____

When do words become "taboo"? _____

_____

According to Bowers and Pleydell-Pearce, what do euphemisms allow people to do?

_____

_____

_____

What three subjects are considered taboo in most of the world?

1. _____   2. _____   3. _____

Provide two ways that language is policed:

_____

Provide an example of political correctness:

_____

What is the most important thing to do when you offend because of your language choice?

_____

_____

Why are phonetic misunderstandings common?

_____

_____

How can you avoid misunderstandings due to phonetic differences?

_____

_____

What are idiomatic expressions? _____

_____

Where can you find help with idiomatic expressions? _____

When is it a good idea to avoid idiomatic expressions? _____

_____

Define the phrase "figurative language": _____

_____

_____

List the seven categories of figurative language AND provide an example of each:

1. _____

_____

2. _____

_____

3. _____

_____

4. _____

_____

5. _____

_____

6. _____

_____

7. _____

_____

Explain syntactic misunderstandings AND give an example of one:

_____

_____

When do the pragmatic elements of language use tend to occur?

1. _____

2. _____

How can you avoid pragmatic misunderstandings in the English language?

_____

_____

When you are learning a language, how can you gain an understanding of the pragmatic elements?

_____

_____

Name: _____   Period: _____

ICC Chapter 4 Journal #1

Circle the category that best describes your current verbal communication skills.

Very Deficient   Deficient   Fair   Good   Excellent   Superior

Explain your evaluation of your verbal communication skills.

_____

_____

_____

_____

_____

Of the four levels of language (phonetics, semantics, syntactics, and pragmatics), on what levels of language are you strongest? Why? (Give examples of your strengths.)

_____

_____

_____

_____

Of the four levels of language, what levels of language give you the most problems? Why? (Give examples of the problems that arise.)

_____

_____

_____

_____

What languages can you understand, speak, or read?

_____

_____

_____

_____

What other languages would you like to learn? Why?

_____

_____

_____

_____

_____

Do you think most people would benefit from learning a second language? Why or why not?

_____

_____

_____

_____

_____

Do you think you are a high context communicator or a low context communicator? Explain your answer.

_____

_____

_____

_____

_____

What are some words that you find to be "taboo?" Why are these words taboo for you?

_____

_____

_____

_____

_____

What subjects or conversational topics do you find to be "taboo?" Why are these subjects or topics taboo for you?

_____

_____

_____

_____

_____

Do you think it is appropriate to control or "police" language? Why or why not?

_____

_____

_____

_____

_____

_____

_____

_____

_____

_____

What should you do when someone tells you that your language has offended them?

_____

_____

_____

_____

_____

_____

What should you do when someone uses language that offends you?

_____

_____

_____

_____

_____

_____

_____

What can you do to improve your verbal communication skills?

_____

_____

_____

_____

Will you take steps to improve your verbal communication skills? Why or why not?

_____

_____

Name: _____   Period: _____

ICC Chapter 4 Quiz

Match the terms with their appropriate definitions.

1. Phonetics _____   2. Semantics _____   3. Syntactics _____

4. Pragmatics _____   5. Tonal languages _____   6. Translation _____

7. Interpretation _____   8. Low context _____   9. High context _____

10. Language families _____   11. Language isolates _____   12. Linguistic relativity _____

13. Linguistic universalism _____   14. Sapir-Worf hypothesis _____

 A. A text transferred from one language to another, with efforts made to maintain the underlying cultur-ally-bound meanings of the original text.
 B. The work of professional interpreters who must instantaneously hear, understand, and transfer infor-mation from one language to another.
 C. The study of language ambiguities that can only be explained through contextual understandings of time, place, relationship, and manner of utterance.
 D. The study of the rules that govern the structure of any language—rules about the ways in which words are put together to form phrases, clauses, or sentences.
 E. The study of the meanings of words and sentences and the relationships between the meanings of words and the meanings of the sentences they exist within.
 F. The study of the sounds of words and the ways we transcribe the sounds of words.
 G. Languages in which meaning is dependent on the combination of word and tone.
 H. Languages that developed in isolation from other languages and share no common root.
 I. Languages that share a common origin.
 J. A communication style that assumes that communicators share a previously established context. As a result, it is unnecessary and often annoying to explain every detail.
 K. A communication style that assumes that communicators do not share a previously established con-text. Thoughts and ideas must be explained clearly.
 L. The notion developed by Brown and Lenneberg that language influences thoughts and behaviors.
 M. The school of thought concerned with the notion that language influences our perceptions in substan-tial ways.
 N. The school of thought concerned with the notion that languages are substantially similar and influ-ence thought in similar ways.

List the four levels of language from simplest to most complex:

15. Level 1 (simplest)   _____   A. Syntactics

16. Level 2   _____   B. Pragmatics

17. Level 3   _____   C. Semantics

18. Level 4 (most complex)   _____   D. Phonetics

19. T. or F.   Approximately 4,000 languages exist in the world today.

20. T. or F.   Almost 300 different languages are spoken in China alone.

21. T. or F.   85% of people in the world today speak languages that are part of the six most common language families.

22. T. or F.   The Basque language is a language isolate.

23. T. or F.   Whereas translation usually refers to translating the spoken word almost instantaneously, interpretation usually refers to translating a written text from one language to another.

24. Which of the following statements about language is true?
    A. Language influences our perceptions.
    B. Language influences our behaviors.
    C. Language influences how we remember events.
    D. All of the above.

25. T. or F.   High context communicators assume that people do not share a previously established communication context.

26. T. or F.   Most people in the United States are low context communicators.

27. Words become _____ in any language when they are used primarily in a provocative or subversive way.

28. T. or F.   Every culture has taboo subjects.

29. T. or F.   In China it is taboo to discuss how much money someone makes.

30. T. or F.   In Nigeria it is taboo to discuss politics and religion.

31. T. or F.   All children in Wales study Welsh until the age of 16.

32. T. or F.   English is the official, federally recognized language of the United States.

33. T. or F.   In China, government publications and signage are provided in five different languages.

34. T. or F.   When you are working with people whose first language is not English, it is a good idea to incorporate idiomatic expressions whenever possible.

35. T. or F.   When you offend someone because of your language choices, one of the last things you should do is apologize, especially if you did not intend to offend anyone.

Name: _____   Period: _____

ICC Chapter 4 Activity Sheet #1

Linguistic Differences and Linguistic Relativity

In Malawi, the names of its largest cities are shortened by locals. Lilongwe is referred to as "L" and Blantyre as "BT," but the one city that is the most confounding to travelers is the city known by locals as "Texas." Insiders hint: "Texas" is actually the small, primarily white, city of Zomba. When we in the United States think of Texas, we think of a large State where people do everything bigger and bolder. In Malawi, a small nation roughly the size of Ohio in southeast Africa, Zomba got the name "Texas" not because of its size but because nothing says white to the people of Malawi like "Texas"(Menkedick 2010).

You don't have to go all the way to Africa to find regional language differences that confound outsiders.

Activity: Finding linguistic differences in the United States

Do a websearch for "22 Maps That Show How Americans Speak English Totally Differently From Each Other"(Hickey 2013). Browse the maps to find the answers to the following questions:

1) What is the deepest linguistic divide in the United States?

_____

_____

2) The second syllable of what word creates deep linguistic schisms?

_____

3) What dessert does everyone in the United States pronounce differently?

_____

4) What are the most common terms for sweetened carbonated beverages by region?

_____

_____

_____

5) What do people from Wisconsin and Rhode Island call a drinking fountain?

_____

6) What do people from Alabama and Mississippi call it when it rains while the sun is shining?

_____

Activity: Linguistic Relativity: Time to speculate!

Now that we know some of the many ways our perceptions are filtered by the language we speak, imagine what would happen if you had a perceptual filter that focused your attention on geometry (an understanding of the measurement and relationships of points, lines, angles, surfaces, and solids). Think back to the Pormpuraaw people's mental maps and what those mental maps allowed them to do; then speculate about 1) how a focus on geometry might manifest in a language, 2) what conditions might make instant mental geometry essential within a language and 3) what instant mental geometry would allow you to do.

1) How might a focus on the principles of geometry manifest in a language (keeping in mind that in order for geometric knowledge to be second nature it would have to be a constant part of daily communication)?

_____

_____

_____

_____

_____

2) What conditions might make instant mental geometry essential within a language?

_____

_____

_____

_____

3) What might instant mental geometry allow you to do?

_____

_____

_____

_____

Name: _____   Period: _____

ICC Chapter 4 Activity Sheet #2

Blame Placing and High/Low Context Communication Styles

Blame Placing

Do a Web search on "to blame news." Look over the news stories. List five stories that clearly show English language users' tendency to focus on agents (people or other specific actors) as the cause of actions.

1. Title of Story: _____

_____

Who is blamed: _____

_____

2. Title of Story: _____

_____

Who is blamed: _____

_____

3. Title of Story: _____

_____

Who is blamed: _____

_____

4. Title of Story: _____

_____

Who is blamed: _____

_____

5. Title of Story: _____

_____

Who is blamed: _____

_____

Activity: High/Low Context Communication Styles

Identify whether each situation is an example of a high context or low context communication style.

Situation #1: Your instructor tells you that you have a research paper coming up in class. The directions include the specific parameters of the question you must answer as well as the font, spacing, running header and footer, margins and bibliography style (as well as examples of the bibliography style).

Situation #1 is an example of a communication that is (circle one): High context or Low Context

Situation #2: You answer the phone, and your friend says only two words: "It's time." Five minutes later, you arrive at your friend's house, ready for a night on the town.

Situation #2 is an example of a communication that is (circle one): High context or Low Context

Situation #3: A mother teaches her child how to wash a window. Mother and child go through each step together while the mother coaches the child through the process.

Situation #3 is an example of a communication that is (circle one): High context or Low Context

Situation #4: You enter a business meeting and the client immediately hands you a business card then stands in silent expectation, without responding to any other discussion, until you offer your business card in return.

Situation #4 is an example of a communication that is (circle one): High context or Low Context

Situation #5: You visit someone's home and, at the entrance, you see shoes lined up outside the door. You remove your shoes as you recognize that is the custom in this home.

Situation #5 is an example of a communication that is (circle one): High context or Low Context

Answers: 1) Low, 2) High, 3) Low, 4) High, 5) High

Chapter Evaluation   Name: _____

Chapter: _____   Class: _____

Most difficult or confusing ideas from the chapter:

1. _____

    _____

    _____

2. _____

    _____

    _____

Most controversial or hard to accept ideas from the chapter:

1. _____

    _____

    _____

2. _____

    _____

    _____

Suggestions for improving the chapter:

1. _____

    _____

    _____

2. _____

    _____

    _____

Most important or useful ideas from the chapter:

1. _____

    _____

    _____

2. _____

    _____

    _____

3. _____

    _____

    _____

Most important chapter skills and/or attitudes to develop:

1. _____

    _____

    _____

2. _____

    _____

    _____

Questions generated by reading the chapter:

1. _____

    _____

    _____

2. _____

    _____

    _____

Chapter 5

Nonverbal Communication

Chapter Learning Objectives

(Check off when you think a learning objective has been achieved.)

1. _____ Clearly distinguish nonverbal communication from verbal communication.

2. _____ Understand and describe five major characteristics of nonverbal communication in order to appreciate the importance of nonverbal communication for intercultural interactions.

3. _____ List and describe 10 general functions of nonverbal communication.

4. _____ Develop an awareness of and sensitivity to cultural differences in 10 specific areas of nonverbal communication.

5. _____ Understand the functions of silence in different cultural settings.

6. _____ Be aware of nonverbal messages related to dining in different cultures.

7. _____ Develop effective habits and practices in order to improve your nonverbal communication.

Workbook Handouts

(Check off when each handout has been completed.)

_____ Chapter 5 Reading Guide (6 pages)

_____ Chapter 5 Journal #1 (6 pages)

_____ Chapter 5 Quiz (2 pages)

_____ Chapter 5 Activity Sheet #1 (Clothing and Adornment Quiz) (2 pages)

_____ Chapter 5 Activity Sheet #2 (Sending Nonverbal Messages) (2 pages)

_____ Chapter 5 Evaluation (2 pages)

Name: _____   Period: _____

ICC Chapter 5 Reading Guide

List AND provide an example of the four different types of human communication:

1. _____

_____

2. _____

_____

3. _____

_____

4. _____

_____

Define the term "paralanguage" AND provide an example:

_____

_____

_____

Explain five characteristics of nonverbal communication.

1. _____

2. _____

3. _____

4. _____

5. _____

List the ten general functions of nonverbal communication:

1. _____

2. _____

3. _____

4. _____

5. _____

6. _____

7. _____

8. _____

9. _____

10. _____

Define "chronemics" and give two examples from around the world.

_____

_____

1. _____

2. _____

Provide the name and actual length for the four different types of "distances" that E.T. Hall discovered and Americans recognize:

1. _____

2. _____

3. _____

4. _____

Provide two examples of proxemics from around the world:

1. _____

_____

2. _____

_____

What is the study of haptics?

_____

_____

Provide two examples of haptics from around the world:

1. _____

   _____

2. _____

   _____

List the four categories that comprise a person's physical appearance:

1. _____   3. _____

2. _____   4. _____

Provide four functions of clothing:

1. _____

2. _____

3. _____

4. _____

Define the term "kinesics":

_____

_____

Provide two examples of kinesics from around the world:

1. _____

   _____

2. _____

   _____

According to the text, what do you need to consider when using hand gestures?

_____

_____

List the six basic emotions communicated with similar facial expressions in all cultures:

1. _____ 4. _____

2. _____ 5. _____

3. _____ 6. _____

Define the term "oculesics": _____

_____

List the four functions of oculesics:

1. _____ 3. _____

2. _____ 4. _____

Provide two examples of oculesics from around the world:

1. _____

_____

2. _____

_____

What is the study of olfactics? _____

_____

Provide two distinct examples of olfactics from around the world:

1. _____

_____

2. _____

_____

What does the study of paravocalics include?

_____

_____

_____

When you learn another human language, of what should you be aware?

_____

_____

Provide two examples of other types of paralanguage from around the world:

1. _____

   _____

2. _____

   _____

Give three functions of silence in America:

1. _____

2. _____

3. _____

Give three functions of silence in other countries:

1. _____

2. _____

3. _____

Provide your favorite proverb about silence, found in the text:

_____

_____

_____

Give three examples of nonverbal communication when dining:

1. _____

   _____

2. _____

   _____

3. _____

   _____

Explain eight ways you can improve your nonverbal communication:

1. _____

   _____

2. _____

   _____

3. _____

   _____

4. _____

   _____

5. _____

   _____

6. _____

   _____

7. _____

   _____

8. _____

   _____

Name: _____   Period: _____

ICC Chapter 5 Journal #1

Do you think verbal or nonverbal communication is more important for intercultural interactions? Explain your answer.

_____

_____

_____

_____

_____

Circle the category that best describes your current nonverbal communication skills.

Very Deficient   Deficient   Fair   Good   Excellent   Superior

Explain your evaluation of your nonverbal communication skills.

_____

_____

_____

_____

_____

The textbook presents five ways nonverbal communication differs from verbal communication. Which of these differences is most important? Explain your answer.

_____

_____

_____

_____

Are you a high context or a low context communicator? Do you rely primarily upon verbal language to communicate your messages, or do you usually combine your verbal language with nonverbal cues? Explain your answer, and give examples of your typical communication behaviors.

_____

_____

_____

_____

_____

The textbook lists ten areas of nonverbal communication: 1) chronemics, 2) proxemics, 3) haptics, 4) personal appearance, 5) kinesics, 6) hand gestures, 7) facial expressions, 8) oculesics, 9) olfactics, and 10) paravocalics.

In which of these 10 areas of nonverbal communication are you especially strong? List at least three of these areas, and give examples that demonstrate your strengths in these areas.

_____

_____

_____

_____

_____

_____

_____

In which of these 10 areas of nonverbal communication are you especially weak? List at least three of these areas, and give examples that demonstrate your weaknesses in these areas.

_____

_____

_____

_____

_____

_____

_____

_____

Are you primarily a monochronic or polychronic person? Explain your answer.

_____

_____

_____

_____

Compared with other Americans, how much personal space do you need, a lot or a little? Explain.

_____

_____

_____

_____

Are you a high-contact or a low-contact person? Do you touch other people often or rarely? Explain.

_____

_____

_____

_____

Do you put a lot of time and effort into your personal appearance? Why or why not?

_____

_____

_____

_____

_____

Do you enjoy displaying your body to others? Why or why not?

_____

_____

_____

_____

Do you fully use your body when communicating with others? Do you often use head movements, torso movements, and leg movements? Why or why not?

_____

_____

_____

_____

Do you "speak with your hands?" Do you use a lot of hand gestures when you communicate? Why or why not?

_____

_____

_____

_____

How expressive is your face? Do you use facial expressions to reveal your emotional states, or do you try to maintain an "inscrutable" facial expression? Explain your answer.

_____

_____

_____

_____

_____

Do you find it difficult or easy to maintain eye contact with other people? Explain your answer.

_____

_____

_____

_____

_____

Do you generally think that body odors are natural or offensive? Explain your answer.

_____

_____

_____

_____

_____

Do you think you speak more quickly or more slowly than most other Americans? Explain your answer.

_____

_____

_____

_____

_____

Do you speak with an accent? If so, what accent do you have?

_____

_____

_____

_____

How comfortable are you with silence? Do you enjoy silence, or do you prefer to have sound and/or conversation occurring almost at all times? Explain your preference for silence or sound.

_____

_____

_____

_____

_____

Do you want to improve your nonverbal communication? Why or why not?

_____

_____

_____

The textbook lists nine tips for improving your nonverbal communication. List the three tips that you think will be most useful or beneficial for you, and make a specific plan to put this tip into practice.

Tip #1: _____

_____

My specific plan: _____

_____

Tip #2: _____

_____

My specific plan: _____

_____

Tip #3: _____

_____

My specific plan: _____

_____

Name: _____   Period: _____

ICC Chapter 5 Quiz

Match the terms with their appropriate definitions.

1. Verbal communication _____   2. Nonverbal communication _____   3. Paralanguage _____

4. Vocal communication _____   5. Nonvocal communication _____   6. Adaptors _____

7. Affect displays _____   8. Emblems _____   9. Illustrators _____

10. Regulators _____   11. Inscrutability _____   12. Posture _____

   A. The way people hold their body when sitting or standing.
   B. Vocal, nonverbal communication elements such as pitch, rate, and volume.
   C. The quality of being difficult to understand or hard to read.
   D. Communication expressed in human language.
   E. Communication expressed through the human voice.
   F. Communication that occurs through means other than the human voice.
   G. Any communication that occurs through means other than human language.
   H. Nonverbal behaviors that help people adapt or adjust to their environment.
   I. Nonverbal cues that signal the emotional state of a communicator.
   J. Nonverbal cues that help control the flow of communication.
   K. Nonverbal symbols that take the place of verbal symbols.
   L. Nonverbal symbols that emphasize or reinforce a verbal message.

13. Chronemics _____   14. Monochronic _____   15. Polychronic _____

16. Proxemics _____   17. Personal space _____   18. Territoriality _____

19. Kinesics _____   20. Oculesics _____   21. Olfactics _____

22. Haptics _____   23. High contact _____   24. Low contact _____

   A. The study of eye behavior, gaze, and eye-related nonverbal communication.
   B. The study of the way people and cultures view and use time.
   C. The study of body movement.
   D. The study of the way people and cultures use space.
   E. The study of the use of touch.
   F. The study of human smell and the use of scents.
   G. People or cultures that view time as a linear entity that can be segmented into precise units.
   H. People or cultures that view time as circular and repeatable and who tend to do several things at once.
   I. People or cultures that prefer a low degree of physical contact and that require personal space.
   J. People or cultures that prefer and are comfortable with a high degree of physical contact.
   K. The area surrounding a person that is perceived as private by that person and who may regard movement into that space as intrusive.
   L. How people use space and other objects to indicate ownership or occupancy of areas.

Match E.T. Hall's distances with their approximate measurements:

25. Personal distance _____   A. touching to 18 inches

26. Public distance _____   B. 4 to 12 feet

27. Social distance _____   C. 12 feet or more

28. Intimate distance _____   D. 18 inches to 4 feet

29. Which of the following statements is *not* true about nonverbal communication?
    A. Nonverbal communication is continuous.
    B. Nonverbal communication is often conscious and intentional.
    C. Nonverbal communication is more believable than verbal communication.
    D. Nonverbal communication is more ambiguous than verbal communication.

30. T. or F.   Verbal communication is used more often than nonverbal communication to send   relational messages.

31. Which of the following statements about nonverbal cues are true?
    A. Nonverbal cues sometimes emphasize or reinforce verbal messages.
    B. Nonverbal cues sometimes replace verbal messages.
    C. Nonverbal cues sometimes regulate the flow of communication.
    D. Nonverbal cues sometimes reveal the inner states of communicators.
    E. All of the above.

32. Which of the following statements about nonverbals are *not* true?
    A. Nonverbals are used to create and communicate our identities.
    B. Nonverbals are used to indicate status.
    C. Nonverbals are used to contradict verbal messages.
    D. Nonverbals are used to communicate verbal messages.
    E. None of the above.

33. Eastern cultures that train people to mask their emotions by keeping what American's call a "poker face" admire the behavioral trait called _____.

34. Verbal and nonverbal messages that communicate how we think and feel about others are called _____ messages.

35. T. or F.   There is not much you can do to improve your nonverbal communication skills: you either know how to communicate nonverbally, or you do not.

Name: _____   Period: _____

ICC Activity Sheet #1

Clothing and Adornment Quiz

Match the following clothing items or adornments with the appropriate description:

ITEM:

1. Ushanka _____   9. Niqab _____   17. Burka _____   25. Babouche _____

2. Sombrero _____   10. Hijab _____   18. Dashiki _____   26. Geta _____

3. Fez _____   11. Turban _____   19. Sarong _____   27. Serape _____

4. Tam _____   12. Keffiyeh _____ 20. Kimono _____   28. Ta moko _____

5. Kufi _____   13. Agal _____   21. Thobe _____   29. Tanga _____

6. Chullo _____   14. Yarmulke _____ 22. Sari _____   30. Kirpan _____

7. Beret _____   15. Payot _____   23. Lava-lava _____ 31. Bindi _____

8. Panama hat _____   16. Parka _____   24. Kilt _____   32. Clog _____

DESCRIPTION:

A. bright red or black dot applied to center of forehead, often worn by women in India
B. skullcap worn by Orthodox Jewish men
C. fur hat worn by Russian men and women
D. skirt worn by Samoan men
E. wooden footwear worn by Dutch and French men and women
F. full face and body covering worn by Muslim women
G. long flowing shirt worn by West African men
H. head covering worn by male Sikhs
I. ankle-length robe worn by Arab men
J. hat worn in Mexico and the Philippines
K. permanent body and face marking of the New Zealand Maori
L. garment worn by Malaysian men and women
M. hat worn by North African men
N. scarf covering the hair of Muslim women
O. hooded fur coat worn by Inuit men and women
P. bikini worn by Brazilian women
Q. hats made and worn by Ecuadorian men
R. sidelocks or sidecurls worn by Orthodox Jewish men and boys
S. garment worn by Indian women
T. covering for head and face worn by Muslim women
U. skullcap worn by West African men
V. skirt worn by Scottish and Irish men

W.   Middle-eastern headdress worn by Arab men
X.   ceremonial sword worn by baptized Sikhs
Y.   full-length robe worn by Japanese women
Z.   Turkish slipper having no heel worn by Muslims in Mosques
AA. long, blanket-like shawl worn by Mexican men
BB. wooden clogs worn by Japanese men and women
CC. cap worn by Basque and French men
DD. woolen cap with ear flaps worn by Andean men and women
EE. cord used to hold the keffiyeh on the head of Arab men
FF. bonnet or cap worn by Scottish men

Answers to Clothing and Adorment Quiz:

ITEM:

1. Ushanka	C	9. Niqab	T	17. Burka	F	25. Babouche	Z
2. Sombrero	J	10. Hijab	N	18. Dashiki	G	26. Geta	BB
3. Fez	M	11. Turban	H	19. Sarong	L	27. Serape	AA
4. Tam	FF	12. Keffiyeh	W	20. Kimono	Y	28. Ta moko	K
5. Kufi	U	13. Agal	EE	21. Thobe	I	29. Tanga	P
6. Chullo	DD	14. Yarmulke	B	22. Sari	S	30. Kirpan	X
7. Beret	CC	15. Payot	R	23. Lava-lava	D	31. Bindi	A
8. Panama hat	Q	16. Parka	O	24. kilt	V	32. Clog	E

Name: _____   Period: _____

ICC Chapter 5 Activity Sheet #2

Sending Nonverbal Messages

Brainstorm and describe how you could send the message "I am romantically attracted to you" using the 10 areas of nonverbal communication:

Chronemics: _____

_____

Proxemics: _____

_____

Haptics: _____

_____

Personal Appearance: _____

_____

Kinesics: _____

_____

Hand Gestures: _____

_____

Facial Expressions: _____

_____

Oculesics: _____

_____

Olfactics: _____

_____

Paravocalics: _____

_____

Brainstorm and describe how you could send the message "I hate you" using the ten areas of nonverbal communication:

Chronemics: _____

_____

Proxemics: _____

_____

Haptics: _____

_____

Personal Appearance: _____

_____

Kinesics: _____

_____

Hand Gestures: _____

_____

Facial Expressions: _____

_____

Oculesics: _____

_____

Olfactics: _____

_____

Paravocalics: _____

_____

Chapter Evaluation   Name: _____

Chapter: _____   Class: _____

Most difficult or confusing ideas from the chapter:

1. _____

_____

_____

2. _____

_____

_____

Most controversial or hard to accept ideas from the chapter:

1. _____

_____

_____

2. _____

_____

_____

Suggestions for improving the chapter:

1. _____

_____

_____

2. _____

_____

_____

Most important or useful ideas from the chapter:

1. _____

_____

_____

2. _____

_____

_____

3. _____

_____

_____

Most important chapter skills and/or attitudes to develop:

1. _____

_____

_____

2. _____

_____

_____

Questions generated by reading the chapter:

1. _____

_____

_____

2. _____

_____

_____

Chapter 6

Approaches to Conflict

Chapter Learning Objectives

(Check off when you think a learning objective has been achieved.)

1. _____ Realize there are different definitions and views of conflict and different cultural approaches to conflict.

2. _____ Understand the different types of conflict.

3. _____ Identify the sources of intercultural conflict.

4. _____ Gain a general knowledge of some of the international conflicts that have occurred.

5. _____ Use an American approach to conflict management based upon five conflict management strategies.

6. _____ Develop other approaches to managing conflict based upon four conflict management styles.

Workbook Handouts

(Check off when each handout has been completed.)

_____ Chapter 6 Reading Guide (4 pages)

_____ Chapter 6 Journal #1 (6 pages)

_____ Chapter 6 Quiz (2 pages)

_____ Chapter 6 Activity Sheet #1 (International Conflicts) (2 pages)

_____ Chapter 6 Evaluation (2 pages)

Name: _____   Period: _____

Chapter 6 Reading Guide

How does a typical American textbook define the term "conflict"?

_____

_____

Provide two examples of how democratic decision-making encourages conflict:

1. _____

_____

2. _____

_____

Explain how conflict is viewed in many traditional collectivistic cultures:

_____

_____

How is the process of bargaining or negotiating a price viewed in other countries?

_____

_____

What should you do if you are trying to resolve a conflict or complete a negotiation with a polychromic person?

_____

_____

Explain what people from Western cultures need to understand when engaged in intercultural conflict.

_____

_____

What does the textbook suggest you do when involved in a conflict with people who care about "face"?

_____

_____

How do some people and cultures view third-party outsiders who are involved in a conflict?

_____

_____

List AND define the 12 types of conflict:

1. _____

2. _____

3. _____

4. _____

5. _____

6. _____

7. _____

8. _____

9. _____

10. _____

11. _____

12. _____

List the 12 different sources of intercultural conflict:

1. _____

2. _____

3. _____

4. _____

5. _____

6. _____

7. _____

8. _____

9. _____

10. _____

11. _____

12. _____

Define the term "genocide" AND provide an example of one major genocide from the twentieth century:

_____

_____

_____

Name three things that may influence people's thoughts and attitudes about America:

1. _____

2. _____

3. _____

List AND describe the five quadrants from Thomas and Kilman's conflict management strategies:

1. _____

2. _____

3. _____

4. _____

5. _____

List AND describe four other approaches to conflict management, the conflict management styles:

1. _____

2. _____

3. _____

4. _____

Provide five tips the textbook presents for interacting with people who have different conflict management styles than your own:

1. _____

_____

2. _____

_____

3. _____

_____

4. _____

_____

5. _____

_____

Provide six tips for effective emotional communication during conflict situations:

1. _____

_____

2. _____

_____

3. _____

_____

4. _____

_____

5. _____

_____

6. _____

_____

Name: _____   Period: _____

ICC Chapter 6 Journal #1

Do you primarily have a positive view of conflict or a negative view of conflict? Explain your answer.

_____

_____

_____

_____

_____

What ideas do you think are valid in the modern, Western, positive view of conflict?

_____

_____

_____

_____

_____

What ideas do you think are invalid or problematic in this positive view of conflict?

_____

_____

_____

_____

What ideas do you think are valid in the traditional, collectivistic, negative view of conflict?

_____

_____

_____

_____

_____

What ideas do you think are invalid or problematic in this negative view of conflict?

_____

_____

_____

_____

Do you enjoy negotiating a price for an item or a service? Why or why not?

_____

_____

_____

_____

Do you work well with deadlines? Why or why not?

_____

_____

_____

_____

When dealing with a conflict, do you think it is appropriate to "separate the people from the problem?" Explain your answer.

_____

_____

_____

_____

What do you think about the concept of "face" that is so important in some cultures? Do you think that this is a valid or important concept? Why or why not?

_____

_____

_____

_____

_____

If you were to use a mediator, would you prefer a neutral third-party outsider or a respected insider? Explain your answer.

_____

_____

_____

_____

Of the 12 types of conflict listed and described in the textbook, which types of conflict have you experienced? Explain your answer.

_____

_____

_____

_____

_____

Of the 12 types of conflict listed in the textbook, which are most serious or harmful? Why?

_____

_____

_____

_____

_____

The textbook lists 12 different sources of intercultural conflict. Give two specific examples of intercultural conflicts in which you have been involved, and identify the source of each conflict.

Example #1: _____

_____

_____

_____

_____

Source of conflict: _____

_____

Example #2: _____

_____

_____

_____

_____

Source of conflict:_____

_____

The textbook lists five major genocides of the twentieth century. What do you think caused these genocides?

_____

_____

_____

_____

_____

_____

_____

What do you think is the general view of America in many countries of the world?

_____

_____

_____

_____

_____

_____

Which countries of the world have the most favorable view of America and Americans?

_____

_____

_____

_____

_____

Which countries of the world have the least favorable view of America and Americans?

_____

_____

_____

_____

_____

Which conflict management strategy do you tend to use the most? Why?

_____

_____

_____

_____

Do you want to use the collaborating strategy more? Why or why not?

_____

_____

_____

_____

The textbook describes four conflict management styles: Discussion Style, Engagement Style, Accommodation Style, and Dynamic Style. What is your primary conflict management style? Why do you prefer this style of conflict management?

_____

_____

_____

_____

_____

To which conflict management style do you have the most difficulty relating? Why?

_____

_____

_____

_____

How effective are you at managing conflict? Explain your answer.

_____

_____

_____

_____

Name: _____   Period: _____

ICC Chapter 6 Quiz

Match the terms with their appropriate definitions.

1. Internecine conflict _____
2. Armed conflict _____
3. Class conflict _____
4. International conflict _____
5. Ethnic conflict _____
6. Historical conflict _____
7. Intrapersonal conflict _____
8. Pseudo conflict _____
9. Serial conflict _____
10. Interpersonal conflict _____
11. Simple conflict _____
12. Escalating conflict _____

A. Conflict that becomes more confrontational, destructive, or serious over time.
B. A political conflict that involves the armed forces of at least one state or factions within a state seeking autonomy or independence.
C. A perceived incompatibility that does not actually exist.
D. Conflict within a group or country.
E. Conflict between two individuals.
F. A psychological struggle created by incompatible or opposing needs, drives, wishes, or demands.
G. Conflict between people of different social or economic classes.
H. Conflict that occurs repeatedly.
I. Conflict between two or more nation states.
J. Disputes between contending groups whose members identify themselves primarily on the basis of ethnicity.
K. Conflict based on past events and memories of past events.
L. An actual incompatibility between two or more interdependent persons or groups.

13. Conflict _____
14. Face _____
15. Genocide _____
16. Accommodating _____
17. Avoiding _____
18. Competing _____
19. Compromising _____
20. Collaborating _____
21. Dynamic style _____
22. Accommodation style _____
23. Engagement style _____
24. Discussion style _____

A. A person's standing or reputation in a community or society.
B. The systematic killing and extermination of a people group because of their race, ethnicity, religion, or cultural practices.
C. A perceived incompatibility between two or more interdependent parties.
D. A conflict style in which people prefer direct and emotionally restrained discussion of conflict.
E. A conflict style in which people prefer direct and emotionally expressive discussion of conflict.
F. A conflict style in which people prefer indirect and emotionally restrained discussion of conflict.
G. A conflict style in which people prefer indirect and emotionally expressive discussion of conflict.
H. People using this strategy work together to create a "win/win" situation for both parties.
I. People using this strategy both yield ground so that a "partial win/partial lose" situation results.
J. People using this strategy give in and allow the other persons to have their way.
K. People using this strategy gain their goals or objectives at the expense of others.
L. People using this strategy do not directly engage in conflict.

25. T. or F.   A positive view of conflict is often held in many modern Western nations.

26. The positive view of conflict is created in part by
    A. the democratic political process.
    B. the adversarial legal system.
    C. decision-making and problem-solving methods used in business.
    D. the value of individualism.
    E. All of the above.

27. T. or F.   A majority of traditional, collectivistic cultures have a very negative view of conflict.

28. The negative view of conflict is created in part by
    A. the value of collectivism.
    B. a high uncertainty avoidance orientation.
    C. a high power distance orientation.
    D. the desire to create group cohesion and group harmony.
    E. All of the above.

29. T. or F.   In many countries, negotiating the price of an item or service is the expected and normal behavior.

30. T. or F.   When negotiating with people from polychronic cultures, you should set firm deadlines.

31. In many Eastern cultures, to be dishonored or disrespected is to suffer a loss of
    _____.

32. T. or F.   The textbook lists about 10 wars or armed conflicts, the United States has been involved in.

33. T. or F.   Compromising is the "win/win" conflict management strategy.

34. The "lose/lose" strategy is the _____ strategy.

35. The conflict management style preferred by most Americans is the
    _____ style.

Name: _____   Period: _____

ICC Chapter 6 Activity Sheet #1

International Conflicts

For each country pair, give a brief description of the historical conflict(s) or tension(s) that exist or have existed between the two countries.

Britain/Ireland: _____

_____

_____

China/Japan: _____

_____

_____

China/Taiwan: _____

_____

_____

China/Tibet: _____

_____

_____

Germany/Russia: _____

_____

_____

India/Pakistan: _____

_____

_____

Israel/Palestine: _____

_____

_____

North Korea/South Korea: _____

_____

_____

Spain/Mexico: _____

_____

_____

United Kingdom/Argentina: _____

_____

_____

United States/Cuba: _____

_____

_____

United States/Iran: _____

_____

_____

United States/Iraq: _____

_____

_____

United States/Japan: _____

_____

_____

United States/Mexico: _____

_____

_____

Chapter Evaluation   Name: _____
Chapter: _____   Class: _____

Most difficult or confusing ideas from the chapter:

1. _____

   _____

   _____

2. _____

   _____

   _____

Most controversial or hard to accept ideas from the chapter:

1. _____

   _____

   _____

2. _____

   _____

   _____

Suggestions for improving the chapter:

1. _____

   _____

   _____

2. _____

   _____

   _____

Most important or useful ideas from the chapter:

1. _____
   _____
   _____

2. _____
   _____
   _____

3. _____
   _____
   _____

Most important chapter skills and/or attitudes to develop:

1. _____
   _____
   _____

2. _____
   _____
   _____

Questions generated by reading the chapter:

1. _____
   _____
   _____

2. _____
   _____
   _____

Chapter 7

Values and Worldviews

Chapter Learning Objectives

(Check off when you think the learning objective has been achieved.)

1. _____ Define values and understand the basic characteristics of values.

2. _____ Identify common pairs of opposing values and determine your personal orientation for each pair of opposing values.

3. _____ Identify common universal questions asked in every human culture, and list the different types of answers given.

4. _____ Distinguish between different basic types of worldviews.

5. _____ Develop a basic understanding of different religious and nonreligious approaches to to living in the world.

6. _____ Describe the values and beliefs of classical world religions.

Workbook Handouts

(Check off when each handout has been completed.)

_____ Chapter 7 Reading Guide (8 pages)

_____ Chapter 7 Journal #1 (American Values) (2 pages)

_____ Chapter 7 Journal #2 (Values Inventory) (2 pages)

_____ Chapter 7 Journal #3 (Worldviews) (4 pages)

_____ Chapter 7 Quiz (2 pages)

_____ Chapter 7 Activity Sheet #1 (World Religions) (2 pages)

_____ Chapter 7 Evaluation (2 pages)

Name: _____   Period: _____

ICC Chapter 7 Reading Guide

Why did Robert Kohls publish the monograph, "The Values American Live By"?

_____

_____

_____

List Kohls' 13 American values and their contrasting traditional values:

1. _____ vs. _____

2. _____ vs. _____

3. _____ vs. _____

4. _____ vs. _____

5. _____ vs. _____

6. _____ vs. _____

7. _____ vs. _____

8. _____ vs. _____

9. _____ vs. _____

10. _____ vs. _____

11. _____ vs. _____

12. _____ vs. _____

13. _____ vs. _____

What does Schwartz' Theory of Basic Values posit?

_____

_____

_____

_____

List Schwartz' six characteristics of values:

1. _____

2. _____

3. _____

4. _____

5. _____

6. _____

According to Schwartz, what are the three universal requirements of human existence?

1. _____

_____

2. _____

_____

3. _____

_____

List Schwartz' ten general human values ranked by order of importance:

1. _____   6. _____

2. _____   7. _____

3. _____   8. _____

4. _____   9. _____

5. _____   10. _____

Explain how these 10 general human values can be contrasted or placed in opposition to each other.

_____

_____

_____

_____

_____

_____

List and describe Hofstede's six cultural value dimensions:

1. _____

_____

2. _____

_____

3. _____

_____

4. _____

_____

5. _____

_____

6. _____

_____

Explain the difference between monochronic and polychronic cultures AND provide an example of each:

_____

_____

_____

_____

_____

What did Clyde Kluckhohn theorize? _____

_____

_____

Provide the five universal questions that Kluckhohn and Strodtbeck posed:_____

1. _____

2. _____

3. _____

4. _____

5. _____

List the five definitions of the term "worldview":

1. _____

   _____

2. _____

   _____

3. _____

   _____

4. _____

   _____

5. _____

   _____

List six characteristics of worldviews:

1. _____

2. _____

3. _____

4. _____

5. _____

6. _____

What is an ontological worldview? _____

_____

_____

List AND describe the three major ontological worldviews:

1. _____

_____

2. _____

_____

3. _____

_____

What is an epistemological worldview? _____

_____

_____

List and describe the three types of epistemological worldviews:

1. _____

_____

2. _____

_____

3. _____

_____

What is a moral/ethical worldview? _____

_____

_____

In what three areas does the moral/ethical worldview attempt to answer questions?

1. _____

2. _____

3. _____

Provide the five definitions for religion:

1. _____

_____

2. _____

_____

3. _____

_____

4. _____

_____

5. _____

_____

List AND define the four elements of religion:

1. _____

_____

2. _____

_____

3. _____

_____

4. _____

_____

Provide a description of the four religious stances:

1. _____

   _____

2. _____

   _____

3. _____

   _____

4. _____

   _____

List AND define the nine religious and nonreligious categories mentioned in the textbook:

1. _____

   _____

2. _____

   _____

3. _____

   _____

4. _____

   _____

5. _____

   _____

6. _____

   _____

7. _____

   _____

8. _____

_____

9. _____

_____

List eight of the classical world religions with which you are <u>least familiar</u> AND their major tenets:

1. _____

_____

2. _____

_____

3. _____

_____

4. _____

_____

5. _____

_____

6. _____

_____

7. _____

_____

8. _____

_____

What are the values and tenets of secular humanism? _____

_____

_____

_____

Name: _____   ' Period: _____

ICC Chapter 7 Journal #1

American Values

After reading through the textbook descriptions of Robert Kohls' thirteen American values, indicate how much each American value plays a part in your personal value system.

American Value	Level of Importance for You				
	Not at all Important	Somewhat Important	Important	Very Important	Extremely
	1	2	3	4	5
1. Personal control over the environment	1	2	3	4	5
2. Change	1	2	3	4	5
3. Time and its control	1	2	3	4	5
4. Equality/Egalitarianism	1	2	3	4	5
5. Individualism/Privacy	1	2	3	4	5
6. Self Help	1	2	3	4	5
7. Competition/Free Enterprise	1	2	3	4	5
8. Future orientation	1	2	3	4	5
9. Work/Action orientation	1	2	3	4	5
10. Informality	1	2	3	4	5
11. Directness/Openness	1	2	3	4	5
12. Practicality/Efficiency	1	2	3	4	5
13. Materialism/ Acquisitiveness	1	2	3	4	5

Do you think Kohls' list of American values applies to American culture today? Why or why not?

_____

_____

_____

List your top five American values, and explain why these values are important to you.

American value #1: _____

Why it is important to me: _____

_____

American value #2: _____

Why it is important to me: _____

_____

American value #3: _____

Why it is important to me:_____

_____

American value #4: _____

Why it is important to me: _____

_____

American value #5: _____

Why it is important to me: _____

_____

Which American values listed by Kohls are not important to you personally? Why?

_____

_____

_____

_____

Are there other important American values that you think Kohls has neglected to mention? If so, what are they?

_____

_____

Name: _____   Period: _____

ICC Chapter 7 Journal #2

Values Inventory

You can use the following value inventory to explore your personal values. We have placed an arrow in the middle of this list of contrasting value pairs so you can analyze and record your personal value preferences. For the first twelve pairs, place the number for each pair (numbers 1 through 12) above the line at the appropriate position for your personal value preferences. For the last eleven pairs, place the numbers 13 to 23 below the line at the appropriate position for your value preferences.

For example, for the value pair "achievement vs. benevolence," place the number 1 exactly in the middle of the line if you value achievement and benevolence equally. If you believe personal achievement is more important than benevolence toward others, place the number 1 closer to the "achievement" end of the line. If you believe benevolence is more important than achievement, place the number 1 closer to the "benevolence" end of the line. Similarly, for each value pair, place the corresponding number (2 through 23) at the appropriate point on the line to represent your value preference. (You can see a sample completed value inventory in Chapter 3 of your textbook.)

An Inventory of Contrasting Values

1. Achievement	vs.	1. Benevolence
2. Acquisitiveness	vs.	2. Detachment
3. Action orientation	vs.	3. Being orientation
4. Change	vs.	4. Tradition
5. Competition	vs.	5. Cooperation
6. Directness	vs.	6. Indirectness
7. Equality	vs.	7. Hierarchy
8. Future orientation	vs.	8. Past orientation
9. Hedonism	vs.	9. Conformity
10. High power distance	vs.	10. Low power distance
11. High uncertainty avoidance	vs.	11. Low uncertainty avoidance
12. Honesty	vs.	12. Saving Face

⬅———————————————————➡

13. Individualism	vs.	13. Collectivism
14. Indulgence	vs.	14. Restraint
15. Informality	vs.	15. Formality
16. Long term orientation	vs.	16. Short term orientation
17. Masculinity	vs.	17. Femininity
18. Monochronic time orientation	vs.	18. Polychronic time
19. Personal control of environment	vs.	19. Fate or luck
20. Power	vs.	20. Universalism
21. Pragmatism	vs.	21. Idealism
22. Self-Direction	vs.	22. Security
23. Self-Help	vs.	23. Birthright inheritance

After completing your value inventory, answer the following questions.

For which value pairs is your value preference most unbalanced? (What are the values that you highly prefer over their contrasting values?)

_____

_____

_____

_____

_____

_____

For which value pairs is your value preference most balanced? (What are the contrasting values that you prefer equally? For which value pairs did you place your "x" in the middle of the line?)

_____

_____

_____

_____

_____

_____

Do you think that a good goal is to appreciate contrasting values equally? Explain your answer.

_____

_____

_____

_____

Name: _____   Period: _____

ICC Chapter 7 Journal #3

Worldviews

After reading Chapter 3 of your textbook, do you think worldviews are important? Why or why not?

_____

_____

_____

_____

_____

What is your ontological worldview? Are you a traditional dualist who believes in the interaction between nature and supernature, are you a modern monist who believes that nature is a closed system, or are you a post-modern person who eschews meta-narratives and "Big Picture" thinking? Does your ontological worldview shift between these options, or do you have another view of what is really real? Explain your answer.

_____

_____

_____

_____

_____

_____

After reading through the list of traditional supernatural concepts/realities found in some of the major world religions, do you consider yourself to be traditionally religious? Why or why not?

_____

_____

_____

_____

_____

What is your primary epistemological worldview? Are you a dogmatic, a cynic, or an idealistic skeptic? Do you believe that truth can be known with absolute certainty, or do you believe that truth does not exist, or do you believe that truth is an ideal to strive toward? Do you believe that language can be used to teach the truth to others, or do you believe that language is a game or power play, or do you believe that language should be used to approach the truth? Explain your answer.

_____

_____

_____

_____

_____

_____

_____

Your textbook lists 10 sources of knowledge or beliefs: 1) authority, 2) inspiration, 3) intuition, 4) introspection, 5) experience, 6) experimentation, 7) observation, 8) revelation, 9) testimony, 10) theorizing/thinking. Which of these knowledge sources gives us the most reliable knowledge and the most valuable insights? Which sources do you value the most? Why?

_____

_____

_____

_____

_____

Which of the ten knowledge sources give us the least reliable knowledge and the least valuable insights? Which sources do you value the least? Why?

_____

_____

_____

_____

_____

_____

What is your view of human nature? Are human beings basically good, evil, a mixture of good and evil, or neither good nor evil? Explain your answer.

_____

_____

_____

_____

_____

_____

What is your view of nature? Is the natural world basically good, evil, a mixture of good and evil, or neither good nor evil? Explain your answer.

_____

_____

_____

_____

_____

_____

What is your view of the supernatural? Is the supernatural world basically good, evil, a mixture of good and evil, or neither good nor evil? Explain your answer.

_____

_____

_____

_____

_____

_____

When interacting with people from different cultures and co-cultures, what worldviews do you think you will have the most difficulty relating to or taking seriously? Why?

_____

_____

_____

_____

_____

_____

What are some practical things you can do to become more familiar and comfortable with the different world-views you may encounter when communicating with people from different cultures?

_____

_____

_____

_____

_____

_____

Name: _____   Period: _____

ICC Chapter 7 Quiz

Match each term with its corresponding definition.

1. Worldview _____   2. Monism _____   3. Dualism _____

4. Ontological worldview _____   5. Epistemological worldview _____

6. Modern worldview _____   7. Traditional worldview _____

8. Postmodern worldview _____   9. Dogmatic worldview _____

10. Cynical worldview _____   11. Idealistic/Skeptical worldview _____

   A. An epistemological worldview that rejects the concept of absolute truth and views language as a game or power play.
   B. An epistemological worldview that accepts the notion of absolute truth and certain knowledge and views language as a vehicle to reveal truth to others.
   C. An epistemological worldview that holds that truth exists, but it is difficult to grasp with certainty; consequently, language is used to approach the truth.
   D. As it relates to ontology, the notion that the universe is composed of two realities.
   E. A person's or society's view of truth, knowledge, and belief.
   F. As it relates to ontology, the view that the world is made of one reality.
   G. A person's or society's view of what is really real.
   H. A collection of beliefs about the universe and humanity's place in it.
   I. An ontological worldview promoted by many major world religions that holds that reality is a combination of the natural and supernatural, the material and immaterial.
   J. An ontological worldview that does not recognize any Big Picture concerning reality.
   K. An ontological worldview that recognizes only the natural world as real.

12. Theism _____   13. Atheism _____   14. Agnosticism _____

15. Deism _____   16. Polytheism _____   17. Pantheism _____

18. Monotheism _____   19. Secularism _____   20. Secular humanism _____

   A. A philosophical or religious orientation of doubt that reserves committing to firm belief or disbelief in God.
   B. Disbelief in, and the denial of, the existence of God or gods.
   C. Belief in the existence of God (or gods), especially in a personal God as the creator and ruler of the universe who is actively involved in the world.
   D. The belief in a creator God who does not intervene in the universe.
   E. The belief in a single, all-powerful God.
   F. The belief that God is in all, including nature.
   G. The belief in many gods or spirits.
   H. Humanism viewed as a system of values and beliefs that are opposed to the values and beliefs of traditional religions.
   I. Indifference to or the rejection of religion and religious practices and considerations.

21. Principles or standards of behavior based on what one views as good or bad, right or wrong, important or unimportant are called _____.

22. T. or F.   Our values guide our decisions about what we should or should not do, depending on whether or not our actions will help us reach our goals.

List Shalom Schwartz' top three general human values:

23. _____ 24._____ 25.   _____

26. T. or F.   Human values often come into conflict and oppose or are in tension with one another.

27. T. or F.   Dutch social psychologist Gerard Hofstede has identified 10 value dimensions.

28. T. or F.   People from polychronic cultures often value promptness over socializing.

29. T. or F.   Kluckhohn and Strodtbeck claim that there are three primary answers to five universal questions.

30. A collection of beliefs about life and the universe held by an individual or group is called a
_____.

31. Which of the following statements about worldviews is true?
    A. Worldviews are deep-seated and often unconscious.
    B. Worldviews are anchored by basic core beliefs, assumptions, or presuppositions.
    C. Worldviews can contain internal conflicts or tensions.
    D. Worldviews can clash or conflict.
    E. All of the above.

32. T. or F.   Religions provide answers to some of the most important human questions, and these answers form worldviews from which we derive our values.

33. Four basic elements of religion are
    A. fear, shame, guilt, and anger   B. sin, sacrifice, salvation, and sanctity
    C. family, church, state, and popular culture   D. creed, code, cult, and community

34. T. or F.   Although religions diverge most significantly in their doctrines and dogmas, there is remarkable agreement in the ethical systems or codes of the major world religions.

35. Four religious stances are
    A. doubt, belief, trust, and unbelief   B. fluid, flexible, fixed, and unfixed
    C. exclusivism, inclusivism, pluralism, and syncretism   D. up, down, right, and left

Name: _____   Period: _____

ICC Chapter 7 Activity Sheet #1

World Religions

To deepen your understanding of some major world religions, complete this activity sheet using the information found in Chapter 3 of your textbook.

Religion	Birthplace	Origin date	Founder
1. Baha'i Faith	_____	_____	_____

Adherents	Sacred text(s)	Major Tenets and Values
_____	_____	_____
	_____	_____
	_____	_____

2. Buddhism	_____	_____	_____
_____	_____	_____
	_____	_____
	_____	_____

3. Christianity	_____	_____	_____
_____	_____	_____
	_____	_____
	_____	_____

4. Confuscianism	_____	_____	_____
_____	_____	_____
	_____	_____
	_____	_____

5. Hinduism	_____	_____	_____
_____	_____	_____
	_____	_____
	_____	_____

Religion	Birthplace	Origin date	Founder
6. Islam	_____	_____	_____

Adherents	Sacred text(s)	Major Tenets and Values
_____	_____	_____
	_____	_____
	_____	_____
7. Jainism	_____	_____
_____	_____	_____
	_____	_____
	_____	_____
8. Judaism	_____	_____
_____	_____	_____
	_____	_____
	_____	_____
9. Shinto	_____	_____
_____	_____	_____
	_____	_____
	_____	_____
10. Sikhism	_____	_____
_____	_____	_____
	_____	_____
	_____	_____
11. Taoism	_____	_____
_____	_____	_____
	_____	_____
	_____	_____

Chapter Evaluation   Name: _____
Chapter: _____   Class: _____

Most difficult or confusing ideas from the chapter:

1. _____

_____

_____

2. _____

_____

_____

Most controversial or hard to accept ideas from the chapter:

1. _____

_____

_____

2. _____

_____

_____

Suggestions for improving the chapter:

1. _____

_____

_____

2. _____

_____

_____

Most important or useful ideas from the chapter:

1. _____
   _____
   _____

2. _____
   _____
   _____

3. _____
   _____
   _____

Most important chapter skills and/or attitudes to develop:

1. _____
   _____
   _____

2. _____
   _____
   _____

Questions generated by reading the chapter:

1. _____
   _____
   _____

2. _____
   _____
   _____

Chapter 8

History vs. Histories

Chapter Learning Objectives

(Check off when you think a learning objective has been achieved.)

1. _____ Learn about the work historians do and the types of source material they consult.

2. _____ Describe the reasons some histories are hidden.

3. _____ Describe the many foci of historical research in our multicultural world.

4. _____ Practice history-based intercultural communication skills.

Workbook Handouts

(Check off when each handout has been completed.)

_____ Chapter 8 Reading Guide (4 pages)

_____ Chapter 8 Journal #1 (Your National and Family Histories) (2 pages)

_____ Chapter 8 Journal #2 (Diasporas of Your Heritage) (2 pages)

_____ Chapter 8 Quiz (2 pages)

_____ Chapter 8 Activity Sheet #1 (Last Year as History) (2 pages)

_____ Chapter 8 Activity Sheet #2 (Types of Histories) (2 pages)

_____ Chapter 8 Evaluation (2 pages)

Chapter 8

History vs. Histories

Name: _____   Period: _____

ICC Chapter 8 Reading Guide

What is the job of a historian?

_____

_____

_____

List AND give an example of the four types of materials historians use to build their narratives:

1. _____

    _____

2. _____

    _____

3. _____

    _____

4. _____

    _____

According to the textbook, give an example of a hidden history:

_____

_____

_____

_____

According to feminists, why don't we learn these stories (hidden histories)?

_____

_____

_____

_____

According to Winston Churchill, why was history written for thousands of years by "the victors"?

_____

_____

_____

What is meant by the term, "national history"? Give an example.

_____

_____

_____

_____

Explain the difference between a political history and a federal history:

_____

_____

_____

_____

On what are colonial histories centered? _____

_____

_____

_____

Define the term "diaspora":_____

_____

_____

List AND provide an example of the five types of diasporas:

1. _____

_____

2. _____

_____

3. _____

_____

4. _____

_____

5. _____

_____

According to the textbook, what blanket assumption should we avoid when considering the history of people of African descent?

_____

_____

_____

To what did the erasure of race lead many brown-skinned Latinos? _____

_____

_____

What do ethnic histories often point out? _____

_____

_____

Provide the name of three ethnic groups that were interred by the US government:

1. _____

2. _____

3. _____

What three dangerous gender biases are promoted in most popular academic history texts?

1. _____

   _____

2. _____

   _____

3. _____

   _____

According to the text, what do socioeconomic class histories draw attention to?

_____

_____

What results when possible histories are obscured or erased?

_____

_____

_____

At what other time are experiences also lost?

_____

_____

List the six suggestions for building your history skills:

1. _____

2. _____

3. _____

4. _____

5. _____

6. _____

Name: _____   Period: _____

ICC Chapter 8 Journal #1

Your National and Family Histories

Write out a brief one-paragraph history of the United States. Be prepared to read this history out loud in class.

_____

_____

_____

_____

_____

_____

_____

_____

_____

What is emphasized or stressed in your brief US history?

_____

_____

_____

_____

_____

What is de-emphasized or omitted from your brief U.S. history?

_____

_____

_____

_____

Write out a brief one-paragraph history of your family. (What are the facts and stories that family members share about the family?) Be prepared to read this history out loud in class.

_____

_____

_____

_____

_____

_____

_____

_____

_____

_____

What is emphasized or stressed in your brief family history?

_____

_____

_____

_____

What is de-emphasized or omitted from your brief family history?

_____

_____

_____

_____

Name: _____   Period: _____

ICC Chapter 8 Journal #2

Diasporas of Your Heritage

Describe in a few sentences your racial, ethnic, or national heritage (choose the one that might be the easiest to trace).

_____

_____

_____

_____

_____

_____

Open a search engine and type in some key words that best represent the above heritage, then add the word "diaspora." Read through some of the entries regarding the ways people of your heritage have been displaced through the centuries. Answer the following about the diasporas of people of your heritage.

1. Roughly how many people of your heritage are counted as having suffered diasporas?

    _____

2. When were people of your heritage displaced (include up to three diasporas)?

    _____

    _____

    _____

    _____

3. What nations have people of your heritage immigrated to as a result of diasporas?

    _____

    _____

_____

_____

4. Using the list of types of diasporas, describe the ways that people of your heritage have been displaced. In cases where the type of displacement doesn't apply, write "N/A."

Victim Diaspora: _____

_____

_____

_____

Labor Diaspora: _____

_____

_____

_____

Imperial Diaspora: _____

_____

_____

_____

Trade Diaspora: _____

_____

_____

_____

Deterritorialized Diaspora: _____

_____

_____

_____

Name: _____   Period: _____

ICC Chapter 8 Quiz

Match each term with its corresponding definition.

1. History _____   2. National history _____   3. Political history_____

4. Federal history _____   5. Colonial history _____   6. Oral history _____

7. Folklore _____   8. Diasporas _____   9. Imperial diasporas _____

10. Labor diasporas _____   11. Trade diasporas _____   12. Victim diasporas _____

13. Deterritorialized diasporas _____   14. Erasure _____

   A. The stories, usually oral, told from generation to generation that transmit the experiences of earlier generations.
   B. Firsthand accounts of historical events as told by the people who experienced them.
   C. The study of past events, especially in relation to human affairs.
   D. History concerned with the pivotal events in a nation that are connected to the governing bodies and officials of a nation.
   E. History concerned with the great events, leaders, values, and beliefs that shape a national identity.
   F. History concerned with providing accurate accounts of federal agencies and the work that they accomplish.
   G. History concerned with the expansion of nations beyond their own borders and the effect those expansions had on indigenous people.
   H. Dispersals of people from their homelands, often traumatically, to two or more foreign lands.
   I. Dispersals of people from their homelands that happen when people are forced from their homes and do not recover their land due to hostile conditions. They still hold a connection to their place of origin; but the recovery of homeland has been deferred indefinitely and displaced by newer centers of religious, cultural and economic achievement.
   J. Dispersals of people from their homelands as a result of being banished from their place of origin usually as a result of conquest, persecution, enslavement, genocide, or exile.
   K. Dispersals of people from their homelands as a result of indentured servitude, enslavement, or need for work as migrant laborers in a foreign land.
   L. Dispersals of people from their homelands by their own choice. These migrants go to another land that has been conquered by their own nation.
   M. Dispersals of people from their homelands, by their own choice, when a community goes abroad to trade in a host society.
   N. An umbrella term used to generally describe instances where the contributions of a person or group of people are erased from the story.

14. T. or F.   Folklore is the traditional, unofficial, non-institutional part of culture.

15. T. or F.   Historians never use folklore to develop their historical narratives.

16. T. or F.   Historians now strive for complete objectivity and a preferred account of events from the past.

17. T. or F.   While many of today's leaders choose to "never forget" in order to avoid the dangers of the past, the history that we tend to honor is still the history of war, oppression, and victory.

18. According to the American Historical Association, diligent historians must
    A. honor the integrity of the historical record.
    B. acknowledge their debts to other historians.
    C. acknowledge and voice their own point of view.
    D. realize that multiple, conflicting perspectives are among the truths of history.
    E. All of the above.

19. To build their historical narratives, historians look to
    A. the public record (news articles, government documents, and Internet sources)
    B. private records (personal correspondence, family photos, etc.)
    C. oral histories (firsthand accounts of historical events)
    D. folklore (stories, usually oral, told from generation to generation)
    E. All of the above.

20. T. or F.   The propensity to assume that everyone is more civilized than they were in the past has obscured our understanding of the way people have been treated throughout history.

21. T. or F.   In 1940, historians in the United States were almost all black females from traditional merchant class families.

22. T. or F.   Today, we have a much wider view of history thanks to the expansion of academic interest in "hidden histories" that began in the 1970s and continues today.

23. T. or F.   According to Jared Diamond, "Much of human history has consisted of unequal conflicts between the haves and the have-nots."

24. A dispersal of people from their homeland, often traumatically, to two or more foreign lands is called a _____.

25. T. or F.   Robin Cohen lays out 10 different types of diasporas.

26. T. or F.   Most often, when we think of "minorities" in the United States, we think of racial groups.

27. T. or F.   The erasure of race leads many brown-skinned Latinos to rejoice.

28. T. or F.   Gender historians have uncovered at least three dangerous biases against women.

29. T. or F.   Socioeconomic class histories draw attention to the class and wealth disparities that propel historic events.

30. T. or F.   The textbook presents at least six things you can do to build skills dealing with history.

Name: _____   Period: _____

ICC Chapter 8 Activity Sheet #1

Last Year as History

Type the last year plus the words "top stories" into a search engine (Example: 2013 top stories). Skim the list of major news stories from last year. Answer the following questions about the stories you saw:

1. What stories were of the most interest to you?

   _____

   _____

   _____

   _____

   _____

   _____

2. Do you think these stories will be remembered 50 years from now? If so, why? If not, why not?

   _____

   _____

   _____

   _____

   _____

   _____

   _____

3. What story do you think is most likely to be remembered as "history" 50 years from now?

   _____

   _____

   _____

   _____

4. Why do you think this story will be remembered 50 years from now?

_____

_____

_____

_____

_____

_____

5. Thinking back to all the stories that you saw as you searched, what made you deem this story "history-worthy" over all the others in your search?

_____

_____

_____

_____

_____

_____

6. What are the politics surrounding this history-worthy story? Search further on the Internet if you are uncertain of the politics surrounding this story.

_____

_____

_____

_____

_____

_____

Name: _____   Period: _____

ICC Chapter 8 Activity Sheet #2

Types of Histories

colonial histories   cultural group histories   diasporic histories   ethnic histories
family histories   gender histories   intellectual histories   national histories
political histories   racial histories   religious histories
sexual orientation histories   socioeconomic class histories

List at least one group's histories that you think was omitted from this list (more if they come to mind):

_____

_____

_____

_____

Why do you think these groups ought to be included?

_____

_____

_____

_____

_____

What might happen to these groups if they are not included?

_____

_____

_____

_____

_____

_____

Choose one of the above history types (either from the printed list or your own list) that reflect your own identity. Write a brief historical narrative of an event that you think should be included in history textbooks.

_____

_____

_____

_____

_____

_____

_____

_____

_____

_____

_____

_____

_____

How can you share this history with others?

_____

_____

_____

_____

Chapter Evaluation

Name: _____

Chapter: _____

Class: _____

Most difficult or confusing ideas from the chapter:

1. _____

_____

_____

2. _____

_____

_____

Most controversial or hard to accept ideas from the chapter:

1. _____

_____

_____

2. _____

_____

_____

Suggestions for improving the chapter:

1. _____

_____

_____

2. _____

_____

_____

Most important or useful ideas from the chapter:

1. _____

_____

_____

2. _____

_____

_____

3. _____

_____

_____

Most important chapter skills and/or attitudes to develop:

1. _____

_____

_____

2. _____

_____

_____

Questions generated by reading the chapter:

1. _____

_____

_____

2. _____

_____

_____

Chapter 9

Our Multifaceted Identities

Student Learning Objectives

(Check off when you think a learning objective has been achieved.)

1. _____ Gain an appreciation of our multifaceted identities.

2. _____ Learn about the pitfalls of stereotyping.

3. _____ Understand the impact of privilege and appreciate the unearned benefits each of us receives as a result of membership in particular groups in our society.

4. _____ Trace our Majority and Minority Development within our own identities.

5. _____ Learn to support other people's identities.

Workbook Handouts

(Check off when each handout has been completed.)

_____ Chapter 9 Reading Guide (4 pages)

_____ Chapter 9 Journal #1 (Circles of My Multicultural Self) (2 pages)

_____ Chapter 9 Journal #2 (Identity Development/Allies) (4 pages)

_____ Chapter 9 Quiz (2 pages)

_____ Chapter 9 Activity Sheet #1 (Stereotypes vs Generalizations) (2 pages)

_____ Chapter 9 Activity Sheet #2 (Check Your Privilege) (2 pages)

_____ Chapter 9 Evaluation (2 pages)

Name: _____   Period: _____

ICC Chapter 9 Reading Guide

Define the term "identity": _____

_____

_____

Explain the two ways we "unpack" the definition of identity:

1. _____

2. _____

List the many ways our lenses for identity are constructed by our experiences:

1. _____

2. _____

3. _____

4. _____

5. _____

6. _____

7. _____

8. _____

9. _____

10. _____

11. _____

Define the term "stereotyping":

_____

_____

_____

What are "subconscious biases"?

_____

_____

What two things are our biases imbedded in? _____

_____

Why are "positive stereotypes" just as harmful as negative stereotypes?

_____

_____

_____

_____

List AND define three microaggressions:

1. _____

   _____

2. _____

   _____

3. _____

   _____

What does Zipf's Law assert? _____

_____

_____

Why do people change the terminology used to describe minorities? _____

_____

_____

What is the danger of having a single story? _____

_____

Define the term "prejudice": _____

_____

Give an example of prejudice: _____

_____

Define the term, "privilege": _____

_____

_____

Give an example of privilege: _____

_____

List nine kinds of privilege in our US society:

1. _____   2. _____   3. _____

4. _____   5. _____   6. _____

7. _____   8. _____   9. _____

What does the phrase "minority identity" mean? _____

_____

List AND provide an example of the four stages of <u>Minority</u> Identity Development:

1. _____

_____

2. _____

_____

3. _____

_____

4. _____

_____

List AND provide an example of the four stages of <u>Majority</u> Identity Development:

1. _____

_____

2. _____

_____

3. _____

_____

4. _____

_____

According to the textbook, what is the "Platinum Rule"?

_____

_____

_____

_____

Name: _____   Period: _____

ICC Chapter 9 Journal #1

Circles of My Multicultural Self*

This activity highlights the multiple dimensions of our identities. It addresses the relationships between our desires to self-define our identities and the social constructions that label us regardless of how we define ourselves.

Place your name in the center circle of the structure to the right. Write an important aspect of your identity in each of the satellite circles an identifier or descriptor that you feel is important in defining you. This can include anything: Asian American, female, mother, athlete, educator, Taoist, scientist, or any descriptor with which you identify.

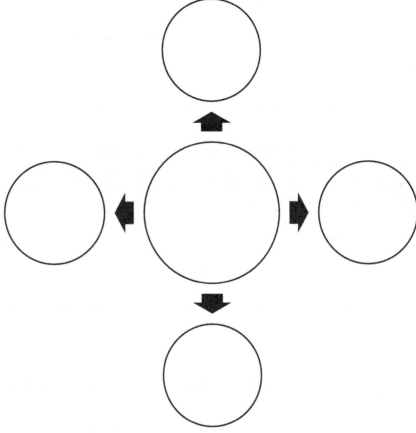

1. Share a story about a time you were especially proud to identify with one of the descriptors you used above.

   _____

   _____

   _____

   _____

2. Share a story about a time it was especially painful to be identified with one of your identifiers or descriptors.

   _____

   _____

_____

_____

Think about your story from #1 in which you were especially proud to be associated with a dimension of your identity. Reframe the story in your mind. This time, before the story begins, the actors in the story have rejected and negated this aspect of your identity. Would the story have unfolded differently? If so, how? If not, why not?

_____

_____

_____

_____

Think about your story from #2 in which it was painful to be associated with the identity dimension you talked about. Reframe the story in your mind. This time, before the story begins, the actors in the story have accepted and supported this aspect of your identity. Would the story have unfolded differently? If so, how? If not, why not? Re-imagine the story below.

_____

_____

_____

_____

Name a stereotype associated with one of the groups with which you identify that is not consistent with who you are. Fill in the following sentence:

I am (a/an) _____ but I am NOT (a/an)_____.

(So if one of my identifiers was "Asian American," and I thought a stereotype was that all Asian Americans are bad drivers, my sentence would be: I am an Asian American, but I am NOT a bad driver.)

*used with permission. Paul C. Gorski, Founder, Ed. *Change and the Multicultural Pavilion*. http://www.ed-change.org/multicultural/activities/circlesofself.html

Name: _____   Period: _____

ICC Chapter 9 Journal #2

Identity Development/Allies

We all have Majority and Minority Identities. Look back through the section of the chapter labeled "Unpacking Majority/Minority Identity Development." List your two Minority Identities that have most shaped your view of the world, and then circle the stage of identity development (from Figure 5.20) that best represents your current experience as a member of each minority group.

Minority identity #1: _____

_____

I feel that I am in the following stage of identity development in regard to #1 (circle one):

Unexamined identity   Conformity   Resistance and Separatism   Integration

This stage of identity development best reflects my experience as a member of the minority group I identified in #1 because:

_____

_____

_____

_____

Minority identity #2: _____

_____

I feel that I am in the following stage of identity development in regard to #2 (circle one):

Unexamined identity   Conformity   Resistance and Separatism   Integration

This stage of identity development best reflects my experience as a member of the minority group I identified in #1 because:

_____

_____

_____

_____

Most of us don't spend much time pondering our majority identities, and all of us have some majority identities. In fact, these identities are usually fairly invisible to us. After reading the section of the chapter about majority/minority identity development, list the 2 majority identities that have most shaped your view of the world, and then circle the stage of identity development (from Figure 5.20) that best represents your current experience as a member of each majority group:

Majority identity #1: _____

_____

I feel that I am in the following stage of identity development in regard to #1 (circle one):

Unexamined identity   Acceptance   Resistance   Redefinition and Reintegration

This stage of identity development best reflects my experience as a member of the majority group I identified in #1 because:

_____

_____

_____

_____

Majority identity #2 _____

_____

I feel that I am in the following stage of identity development in regard to #2 (circle one):

Unexamined identity   Acceptance   Resistance   Redefinition and Reintegration

This stage of identity development best reflects my experience as a member of the majority group I identified in #2 because:

_____

_____

_____

_____

Read the section of the chapter labeled "Support for others' identities." Look back at the minority identities you listed in the first part of this activity. Who, in your life, has acted as an ally in their support of these two aspects that make up an important part of the person you are?

Minority Identity #1 allies: _____

_____

_____

Minority Identity #2 allies: _____

_____

_____

Look back at the majority identities you listed in the first part of this activity. List at least two minority identities that are the counterparts to this majority identity. (Example regarding the US citizen majority identity: permanent worker, immigrant, resident alien, nonimmigrant on student or work visa, undocumented person, DREAMers)

Majority Identity #1 _____

_____

Corresponding minority Identities _____

_____

_____

_____

Majority Identity #2 _____

_____

Corresponding minority Identities _____

_____

_____

_____

Do you have friends who are from any of the minority groups you listed above?   Yes / No

Choose and list one of the minority identities you listed above _____

_____

List three choices you might make in order to act as an ally to someone who is from the minority group you listed:

1. _____

_____

_____

2. _____

_____

_____

3. _____

_____

_____

Name: _____   Period: _____

ICC Chapter 9 Quiz

Match the following terms with their appropriate definitions.

1. Identity _____
2. Majority identity _____
3. Minority identity _____
4. Privilege _____
5. Stereotyping _____
6. Subconscious bias _____
7. Microaggressions _____
8. Microassaults _____
9. Microinsults _____
10. Microinvalidations _____
11. Zipf's Law _____

    A. The tunnel vision that blinds us to ideas that are not in the first place position in our minds.

    B. A subconscious short-hand in which we make snap judgments about other people without even thinking about the fact that we are making a decision.

    C. A person's conception and expression of a single facet of their individuality that is linked with a group affiliation.

    D. An identity that, regardless of your racial or ethnic group, is not the mainstream identity.

    E. An identity that, regardless of your racial or ethnic group, is the mainstream identity.

    F. The intangible, unearned benefits people get as a result of membership in a majority group.

    G. A preference that has built up in our minds based on our experiences. These preferences are the foundations of the snap judgments that we rely on when we stereotype.

    H. Words and actions that exclude or negate the experiential reality of a person.

    I. Deliberate harmful actions and language choices like displaying a Confederate flag or willfully using slurs against a particular group.

    J. Words and actions that subtly convey rudeness and insensitivity while demeaning a person's identity.

    K. The umbrella term for the emotional stab wounds that result from stereotyping people from a minority. These wounds become more painful when someone from a majority uses the stereotype.

12. T. or F.   We don't think much about our own identities unless we begin to notice, or are made to notice, how particular facets of our identities are similar to or different from those around us.

13. T. or F.   In essence, we all have multiple identities.

14. T. or F.   Over our lifetimes, our identities are remarkably stable and unchanging.

15. T. or F.   Our identities act as lenses through which we see the world.

16. Our identity lenses are constructed out of
    A. our beliefs, values, and behavioral choices.
    B. our understandings and misunderstandings of our own histories.
    C. the mainstream and co-cultural groups to which we belong.
    D. the ways we navigate the social roles available in our cultures and co-cultures.
    E. All of the above.

17. Additionally, our identity lenses are also constructed out of
    A. the ways our physical presence is supported/negated by our cultures and co-cultures.
    B. our personal interests, abilities, and desires.
    C. the ways people we care about treat us.
    D. our personal awareness of the many internal agreements/contradictions created by all of our different identities.
    E. All of the above.

18. T. or F.   There are times when our identity lenses create blinders that stop us from seeing experiences beyond the identities that we are focusing on in the moment.

19. T. or F.   We all stereotype. We have biases, and often we aren't aware of these biases, much less that we act based upon them.

20. T. or F.   Often we are completely unaware how our subconscious biases affect the ways we think about ourselves or treat other people.

21. T. or F.   Even when people in the majority don't mean to be cruel, "pin pricks" caused by stereotyping build up over time and create festering wounds.

22. T. or F.   It appears that we only have room in our heads for the first five items in any category that we have created.

23. An unfair feeling of liking or disliking not based in logic or reason is called

_____

24. The intangible, unearned benefits people get as a result of membership in a majority group is called _____.

25. T. or F.   In the United States, just being white tends to provide an economic boost.

List the four stages of majority identity development in the correct order:

26. Stage one   _____   A. Resistance

27. Stage two   _____   B. Acceptance

28. Stage three   _____   C. Unexamined Identity

29. Stage four   _____   D. Redefinition and Reintegration

30. T. or F.   For both majority and minority identities, the unexamined identity stage is characterized by lack of exploration of identity.

Name: _____   Period: _____

ICC Chapter 9 Activity Sheet #1

Stereotypes vs Valid Generalizations

Some tips to help you distinguish valid generalizations from stereotypes:

1) *valid generalizations are qualified with words and phrases such as "most," "many," "the majority of," "often," "generally," etc., whereas invalid stereotypes use or imply universal terms such as "all," "every," "always," "never," etc.*

2) *valid generalizations are based upon evidence, whereas invalid stereotypes are assumed and applied without evidence.*

Identify the valid generalizations with a (V), and the stereotypes with an (S):

1) _____ Many Japanese people have difficulty pronouncing English "Rs" and "Ls" because there are no similar sounds in their language.

2) _____ Illegal immigrants are stealing our jobs.

3) _____ As people move into their 70s and 80s, there is often a dramatic decline in bone density, motor skills, vision and hearing. As a result, people over the age of 70 who drive regularly are more likely to be involved in car accidents.

4) _____ Italians are all connected to the mob.

5) _____ Politicians act unethically as a result of the pressures of running for office, the constant attentions of lobbyists, and their distance from their constituents.

6) _____ Canadians are more polite than US citizens.

7) _____ The Russians are a violent people.

8) _____ Men are stronger than women.

9) _____ The majority of Americans are materialistic.

10) _____ Many Latin Americans are high contact people.

Practice adding appropriate qualifiers to the following statements in order to make them valid generalizations rather than invalid stereotypes.

(Possible Qualifiers: most, many, the majority of, generally, often, a large percentage of)

1. _____ Americans value individualism and privacy.

2. _____ people who live near the equator are high contact.

3. _____ Russians are fatalistic.

4. _____ masculine men value competition.

5. _____ women like to go shopping.

6. _____ young people prefer change.

7. _____ older people are less concerned about pleasing people.

8. _____ people from Asia are concerned about saving face.

9. _____ Mexicans are Catholic.

10. _____ practicing Catholics go to Mass regularly.

Write out a valid generalization:

1. _____

_____

Why do you think this generalization is valid? _____

_____

_____

Write out an invalid stereotype:

1. _____

_____

Why is this stereotype invalid? _____

_____

_____

Name: _____   Period: _____

ICC Chapter 9 Activity Sheet #2

Check Your Privilege

Check your privilege: Gender

Regardless of your gender, please complete the checklist below.

In order to avoid being **sexually assaulted**, I:

_____ check my clothing to make sure it isn't provocative
_____ carry pepper spray
_____ never/rarely walk alone at night
_____ always walk with purpose
_____ always note where the nearest exit is
_____ always tell someone where I am going
_____ keep my keys between my fingers in parking lots and on the street
_____ check the backseat of my car before I get in
_____ never park next to vans
_____ avoid wearing headphones so I can remain alert at all times
_____ always make sure my cell phone is charged
_____ have 911 on speed dial
_____ immediately turn and lock my door as I enter my home
_____ never go on a date with anyone I don't know well
_____ always take friends with me to social events, and stick with them throughout the evening
_____ never leave my drink unattended
_____ have taken self-defense classes

Every day, I:

_____ worry that I might be sexually assaulted

If you checked more than five items on the above list, you likely identify as a woman. If much of the list seemed overly sensitive and a little unbelievable, you may have just experienced male/masculine privilege. Women in the United States, especially feminine women, have been trained to believe that they are in constant danger from sexual predators, whereas most men have been taught none of the above (except to watch their drinks so they don't get robbed). This is just one area in which men tend to have intangible benefits that they are unaware of.

Check your privilege: Race

The checklist below is adapted from Peggy McIntosh's *White Privilege: Unpacking the Invisible Knapsack* (McIntosh, 1988). Retrieved from New York Model for Batterer Programs website: http://nymbp.org/reference/WhitePrivilege.pdf.

When I go shopping:

_____ I can shop anywhere without someone following me around the store or accusing me of theft
_____ I can walk into any hairdresser's shop knowing that someone there will be able to deal with my hair
_____ I can walk into any supermarket and find the foods I grew up with
_____ When I ask to speak to the person in charge, I am usually greeted by someone of my own race
_____ I can buy "flesh colored" band-aids that don't contrast with my skin.

In the media:

_____ I can see people of my own race anytime I turn on the TV or open a magazine
_____ When I watch children's programs I always see people of my own race

In school:

_____ I learned about histories that taught me about my own heritage
_____ I was taught about the founders of our country, all of whom were of my race
_____ I learned that my race exists
_____ I learned that people of my race made this country what it is today
_____ I saw pictures of people of my race in all of my textbooks
_____ I was never asked to speak for people of my racial group
_____ I can walk into any classroom on campus and know that the majority of students share my race
_____ I can enroll in almost any class on campus and be assured that most of my professors will share my race

Financially:

_____ I can walk into any bank and, as long as I have a good credit and banking history, be assured that I can get a loan
_____ I can rent an apartment anywhere as long as I have good credit.

Personally, I am not made to feel that it is a reflection on my race if:

_____ I have body odor issues
_____ my body shape is different from mainstream expectations
_____ I am late to a meeting
_____ I openly discuss race
_____ I excel in a challenging situation

When I drive:
_____ I can drive anywhere I want to without the police pulling me over for being in the wrong place
_____ I don't get pulled over regularly just because there is an All Points Bulletin out for someone of my description
_____ I can drive at 5-10 MPH over the speed limit most of the time without fear of being pulled over

If you checked most of the above, you quite likely identify as white (and you might come from a middle-class background).

Chapter Evaluation

Chapter: _____

Name: _____

Class: _____

Most difficult or confusing ideas from the chapter:

1. _____

_____

_____

2. _____

_____

_____

Most controversial or hard to accept ideas from the chapter:

1. _____

_____

_____

2. _____

_____

_____

Suggestions for improving the chapter:

1. _____

_____

_____

2. _____

_____

_____

Most important or useful ideas from the chapter:

1. _____

_____

_____

2. _____

_____

_____

3. _____

_____

_____

Most important chapter skills and/or attitudes to develop:

1. _____

_____

_____

2. _____

_____

_____

Questions generated by reading the chapter:

1. _____

_____

_____

2. _____

_____

_____

Chapter 10

Intercultural Communication Across Contexts

Chapter Learning Objectives

(Check off when you think a learning objective has been achieved.)

1. _____ Identify and distinguish between travel and different types of tourism.

2. _____ Understand what it takes to be a good guest in foreign countries and a good host to travellers and tourists.

3. _____ List and describe the different health care systems around the world.

Workbook Handouts

(Check off when each handout has been completed.)

_____ Chapter 10 Reading Guide (6 pages)

_____ Chapter 10 Journal #1 (4 pages)

_____ Chapter 10 Quiz (2 pages)

_____ Chapter 10 Activity Sheet #1 (Improving Intercultural Relationships) (4 pages)

_____ Chapter 10 Activity Sheet #2 (Channels of Communication) (2 pages)

_____ Chapter 10 Activity Sheet #3 (Communication Faux Pas) (2 pages)

_____ Chapter 10 Activity Sheet #4 (Reflection For Travel Abroad) (2 pages)

_____ Chapter 10 Activity Sheet #5 (Popular Culture and Perceptions) (2 pages)

_____ Chapter 10 Activity Sheet #6 (Top 10 Nonverbal Behaviors) (4 pages)

_____ Chapter 10 Activity Sheet #7 (Top 10 Words or Phrases) (4 pages)

_____ Chapter 10 Activity Sheet #8: Bridging the Gap Between Health Professionals and Patients (2 pages)

_____ Chapter 10 Evaluation (2 pages)

Name: _____ Period: _____

Chapter 10 Reading Guide

What two characteristics often define communication competency?

1. _____ 2. _____

According to the textbook, what are the five commitments that people interested in becoming competent communicators must adopt?

1. _____

_____

2. _____

_____

3. _____

_____

4. _____

_____

5. _____

_____

Since intercultural couples are more stigmatized and scrutinized what are they more likely to experience from their surrounding communities? _____

_____

_____

_____

How does the similarity principle draw intercultural couples together? _____

_____

_____

_____

List and explain the three categorized strategies that intercultural couples use to resolve their differences.

_____

_____

_____

List and explain the 10 tips for a happier intercultural relationship.

1. _____

2. _____

3. _____

4. _____

5. _____

6. _____

7. _____

8. _____

9. _____

10. _____

Explain the difference between travel and tourism:

_____

_____

_____

_____

Define the term "eco-toursim": _____

_____

_____

_____

What is "medical tourism"? _____

_____

_____

_____

Define the phrase "host culture": _____

_____

_____

What is meant by the term "xenophobia"? _____

_____

_____

Provide five tips for responsible travel and tourism:

1. _____

2. _____

3. _____

4. _____

5. _____

Give three benefits to studying abroad:

1. _____

2. _____

3. _____

Provide five suggestions travelers should consider as they interact with others while abroad:

1. _____

2. _____

3. _____

4. _____

5. _____

Describe what is meant by the phrase "physician-patient relationship" :

_____

_____

Provide the four considerations patients must recognize to be more effective communicators with their physicians:

1. _____

_____

2. _____

_____

3. _____

_____

4. _____

_____

Define complementary medicine

_____

_____

_____

_____

Define alternative medicine

_____

_____

_____

_____

Define and explain the biopsychosocial approach.

_____

_____

_____

_____

List and explain the 5 idiosyncratic and religious factors that healthcare providers often need to consider.

_____

_____

_____

_____

List and explain the 5 factors healthcare consumers consider in their interactions with healthcare providers.

_____

_____

_____

_____

Name: _____   Period: _____

ICC Chapter 10 Journal #1

How many relationships with culturally different people do you have (different race, ethnicities, religions, sexual orientations, degrees of able-bodied-ness, etc.)?

_____

_____

_____

_____

_____

What types of relationships are these (e.g., friends, romantic partners, relatives, acquaintances)? What are some reasons for the network you have developed? How does the concept of proximity discussed in Chapter 10 relate to the network of relationships you have developed?

_____

_____

_____

_____

_____

Have you ever been or are you currently in an *intimate intercultural relationship*? What are some of the challenges and opportunities that are unique to this type of relationship?

_____

_____

_____

_____

_____

The writer of Chapter 10 asserts that intimate intercultural relationships are more stigmatized and scrutinized than traditional ones—do you agree? Why or why not?

_____

_____

_____

_____

The writer of Chapter 10 introduces the idea of *The Romeo and Juliet Effect*. In your opinion, are intercultural couples more likely to grow stronger and closer as a result of external opposition?

_____

_____

_____

_____

_____

In your opinion, which one of the following strategies utilized by intercultural couples to resolve cultural differences is most effective? Why?

1. One-Way Adjustment: One partner accommodates in to the culture of the other.

2. Compromise Adjustment: The couple alternates accommodating (i.e.: family uses different languages in different settings).

3. Creative Adjustment: Couple creates a "third culture" of their own rather than adopting either culture of origin. Their culture may incorporate different aspects of both cultures.

_____

_____

_____

_____

_____

Name: _____   Period: _____

ICC Chapter 10 Journal #2

List the top three countries you would like to visit and briefly explain why you want to visit these countries.

1. _____

   _____

   _____

   _____

2. _____

   _____

   _____

   _____

3. _____

   _____

   _____

   _____

What is holding you back from visiting these countries, and what can you do to overcome these obstacles.

_____

_____

_____

_____

_____

Would you like to study abroad? Why or Why not?

_____

_____

_____

_____

_____

Would you like to host foreign travelers and exchange students? Why or why not?

_____

_____

_____

_____

_____

Would you like to volunteer on a service project in another country? Why or why not?

_____

_____

_____

_____

_____

Name: _____   Period: _____

ICC Chapter 10 Journal #3

Have you ever found yourself reluctant or unable to tell a health professional what you wanted to say? If so, what held you back?

_____

_____

_____

_____

_____

How do your identities influence your health and the way you communicate about it?

_____

_____

_____

_____

_____

Relate one specific example of a time a doctor or other health professional miscommunicated or made an assumption about some aspect of your identity:

_____

_____

_____

_____

_____

_____

How did you feel about the miscommunication or assumption? Why did you feel that way?

_____

_____

_____

_____

_____

What did you do or wish you had done in that moment?

_____

_____

_____

_____

_____

What factors would make it easier for you to communicate more openly with your health professional?

_____

_____

_____

_____

_____

Name: _____ Period: _____

ICC Chapter 10 Quiz

Match the terms with their appropriate definitions.

1. Tourism _____
2. Medical tourism _____
3. Eco-tourism _____
4. Nationality _____
5. Nationalism _____
6. Regionalism _____
7. National character _____
8. Host culture _____
9. Authenticity _____
10. Faux pas _____
11. International students _____
12. Study abroad _____
13. Xenophobia _____
14. Undocumented students _____
15. Self-efficacy _____

A. The dominant culture within a society that a person visits.
B. Extreme fear or hatred of strangers or foreigners.
C. Foreign-born persons attending school in a country who do not have current legal status within that country.
D. Traveling for a specific type of enjoyment and pleasure, often to see sites that have historical or aesthetic significance.
E. A person's belief or perception in their ability or capacity to succeed in certain situations.
F. When traveling, having a mindset to have experiences within a host culture that are true to the lives of the people who live within that culture.
G. Citizenship in the country in which someone is born or is naturalized into.
H. The sense of pride in, patriotic nostalgia for, or devoted commitment to one's nation.
I. A group of characteristics or behavioral traits that apply to the majority population of a whole nation.
J. Communication behaviors that create moments of social awkwardness between people.
K. Foreign nationals on a temporary visa or student visa that are taking courses at an educational institution in a host country.
L. Participation in educational activities while living in a country outside one's country of origin.
M. Traveling to countries where the cost and accessibility of certain medical procedures are more feasible than in one's own country.
N. Traveling for pleasure and enjoyment based on environmental attractions.
O. Devotion for, sense of pride in, and loyalty toward a specific area within a country.

16. T. or F.   Training in workshops and college courses is enough to provide you with communication competence.

17. T. or F.   Communication competency is a constant struggle and a "process of becoming."

18. T. or F.   Personal discovery and transformation is the drive behind most travel.

19. T. or F.   One doesn't have to partake in tourism to travel, but one has to travel to participate in tourism.

20. T. or F.   Eco-tourism and medical tourism are basically the same thing.

21. Travelers might encounter people or cultures that have _____, an extreme fear or hatred of strangers or foreigners.

22. Five tips for responsible travel and tourism are to 1) be informed, 2) be aware, 3) be prepared, 4) be open, and 5) be _____.

23. The benefit of studying abroad is
    B. intercultural development.
    C. educational attainment.
    D. career attainment.
    E. All of the above.

24. An international service organization that sends Americans to all parts of the world is called The _____ _____.

25. T. or F.   Education in the United States is superior to the education in other countries.

Match the following to their appropriate descriptors.

26. T. or F.   In 2015, one in ten U.S. marriages were between individuals of different races and/or ethnicities.

27. T. or F.   Research has shown that intercultural couples marry for the same reasons that traditional couples do: simply because they like each other.

28. Intercultural couples rate which of the following as top issues?

    A. influence of extended family
    B. values and customs
    C. language and communication
    D. gender roles
    E. All of the above.

29. The strategy intercultural couples use to resolve their cultural differences is

    A. one-way adjustment
    B. compromise adjustment
    C. creative adjustment
    D. All of the above.
    E. None of the above.

30. Intercultural couples who experience an increase in external opposition may grow stronger due to the _____ and _____ effect.

31. T. or F.   Western or conventional medicine predominates in the United States.

32. T. or F.   There is no place for alternative or holistic medicine in America.

33. T. or F.   Some co-cultures in America may view sickness and healing primarily as religious issues, rather than medical issues.

34. T. or F.   Physicians are 100 percent responsible for their communication with their patients.

35. T. or F.   Self-efficacy is an important concept for patients approaching their physicians.

ICC Chapter 10 Activity Sheet #1

Improving Intimate Intercultural Relationships

Ten Tips for a Happier Intercultural Romantic Relationship:

1. Commitment to relationship
2. Ability to communicate
3. Sensitivity to other's needs
4. A liking for the other's culture
5. Flexibility
6. Solid, positive self-image
7. Love
8. Common goals
9. Spirit of adventure
10. Sense of humor

Review the section "Skill Builders: Ten Tips for a Happier Intercultural Romantic Relationship." Read each statement by individuals in intimate intercultural relationships below and select which relational tip (above) would be the most helpful in resolving the couple's concern.

_____ "My wife and I were raised completely different. Growing up, my mother used to tell me 'Don't worry so much about what other people think.' My wife remembers her mother saying, 'You can't do that, what would other people think?'"

_____ "I miss genuine friends. I have some friends here, but we have a hard time finding friends that both my husband and I can truly connect with."

_____ "My in-laws feel that my husband should have married a Venezuelan girl. They think I can't understand the culture, cook Venezuelan food, or properly look after my husband. They accept me because they have to but I wouldn't have been their first choice."

_____ "It has been nearly 20 years since I got married and moved here, but I will always think of Argentina as my home."

_____ "In my wife's culture, the extended family is considered equal to the Western notion of the nuclear family. My in-laws want to be involved in every decision we make. I wasn't raised this way and sometimes it can be overwhelming for me."

_____ "Where I come from there is so much interracial mixing that people don't even think about it. Here race is everything and our daughter is interracial. We know she will have to learn how to deal with that. Most people see her as black, not Colombian, not white, not biracial, and simply black."

_____ "Being in an intercultural relationship has opened up my world, taught me to adapt, and become more open-minded to difference. I think I have learned to be more considerate and caring with people around me and I'm more likely to think outside of the Western mindset only."

The 10 tips for happier intercultural romantic relationships benefit any close relationship. Think about your most intimate relationship (friend, family, or partner). Whether or not this is an intercultural relationship, list the top three tips for a happier intercultural romantic relationship that would most benefit your relationship and explain why each would improve the quality of your relationship.

1st tip: _____

Why this tip would improve the quality of my most intimate relationship:

_____

_____

_____

_____

2nd tip: _____

Why this tip would improve the quality of my most intimate relationship:

_____

_____

_____

_____

3rd tip: _____

Why this tip would improve the quality of my most intimate relationship:

_____

_____

_____

_____

Name: _____   Period: _____

ICC Chapter 10 Activity Sheet #2

Channels for Communication

When traveling or living in a foreign country, contact with home is an important ingredient to avoid getting homesick and experiencing culture shock. It would be ethnocentric to assume that a host culture will have the same channels of communication as those found in one's home country. International calling plans can be quite expensive and unrealistic, especially for people living abroad for the first time, so it is important to consider the channels of communication available to you.

In this activity, you are going to explore the different channels of communication you have available to you to make contact with the people at home during your time abroad. In the space provided below, identify three channels of communication that you plan to use during your time abroad to connect with people at home. In addition, identify any barriers that may stand in your way when depending on these channels of communication.

Example:

Internet; specifically Facetime: I am a Mac user and with that come some great applications such as Facetime that can be used to connect with others. It is a great way to both talk to and see my closest friends and family from back home. However, as convenient as this application is, it may be unrealistic because of the time difference in the country that I am visiting (Singapore) and very expensive to have reliable high-speed Internet in my flat/apartment/room.

1. _____

   _____

   _____

   _____

2. _____

   _____

   _____

   _____

3. _____

   _____

   _____

   _____

Now that you have identified communication channels you plan to use, do some research on the country you are visiting and find other potential ways to communicate with people back home. In addition to sources on the Internet, travel guides and travel books may be helpful for discovering new communication channels that may be available within this country.

Example:

0

Although this isn't popular in my small community in the Central Valley of California, Internet cafes are very popular in Japan. This option may give me the opportunity to have the video calling I am looking for to speak with and see my loved ones from home. These cafes are relatively inexpensive and I look forward to potentially using these sites in my future travel to Japan.

_____

_____

_____

_____

_____

_____

_____

_____

_____

_____

_____

_____

_____

_____

_____

_____

Name: _____   Period: _____

ICC Chapter 10 Activity Sheet #3

Communication Faux Pas

One of the most interesting things people encounter when traveling abroad are the differences in communication practices and behaviors among people. Slight differences in mannerisms and etiquette can create moments of confusion and conflict. The term *faux pas* refers to communication behavior that creates moments of social awkwardness between people. When people commit communication faux pas in intercultural settings, they can be interpreted in different ways by people from the host culture. In the best case scenario, these faux pas are swept under the rug, ignored, or forgiven; in the worst case scenario, these faux pas are viewed as being totally disrespectful, and they create ill-will and negative evaluations.

Before traveling abroad, people should research the communication expectations of the host culture they are visiting. For example, if someone were traveling to India, they should know that in India it is considered rude to pass objects with the left hand, and they should know that Indians expect conservative dress for both men and women. Without this knowledge, there is a much greater chance of committing a faux pas.

Select a country that you are interested in traveling to and search the Internet for communication faux pas, cultural etiquette, or expected communication behaviors within that country. Find five distinct faux pas, list them here, and explain how members of the host culture interpret that specific behavior.

Here is an example from a student who researched Thailand:

Touching someone, especially children, on the head is very inappropriate. In Thailand, it is considered not just rude but spiritually taboo to touch someone, especially children, on the head. A person's head is considered sacred, so touching a person's head or even passing over people who are seated can be viewed as inconsiderate and disrespectful.

Now it's your turn. Research five different faux pas and explain their meaning and/or history.

1. _____

   _____

   _____

   _____

   _____

2. _____

   _____

   _____

3.

4.

5.

Name: _____   Period: _____

ICC Chapter 10 Activity Sheet #4

Reflection for Travel Abroad

Throughout your Intercultural Communication textbook, you have learned about important theories, principles, and concepts that should inform effective intercultural communication. However, the information shared in a textbook is only as good as the effective use of this information through skillful implementation.

There is no better time than traveling abroad to put into practice the ideas presented in your textbook. In the space provided below, please identify three theories, principles, or concepts that you believe will be especially helpful when communicating in a foreign country. In addition to identifying the theory, principle, or concept, please explain why you believe this information will be helpful in your interactions with people from other cultures.

Example:

I believe the concept of <u>cultural empathy</u> will be especially helpful when traveling overseas because no doubt I will encounter cultural practices and behaviors that are foreign to me and on some level challenge my preferences and beliefs. Trying to step into the shoes/moccasins/dirt of the people within their culture will help temper my initial bias and potentially open me up for new understanding and appreciation of behaviors unfamiliar to me.

1. _____

_____

_____

_____

_____

_____

_____

_____

_____

_____

_____

2. _____

3. _____

Name: _____   Period: _____

ICC Chapter 10 Activity Sheet #5

Popular Culture and Perceptions of Foreign Countries

The cultures that we are a part of shape our perceptions of the world, including our understanding of foreign countries and the cultures within them. Movies, music, magazine and print media, fashion, social media, and other forms of popular culture help us form a perception of people and cultures in other nations. It is important to analyze and evaluate popular culture in order to understand how it informs and forms our biases. This is especially true before traveling to other countries that have been depicted in certain ways in popular culture.

1. Select a country or a culture of interest outside of your home country.

2. Identify a popular culture artifact that depicts the country or culture of interest.

3. Identify whether this depiction is positive or negative, and consider how this popular culture depiction could influence someone's understanding of this culture if passively accepted as true.

Please repeat these three steps for four different popular culture artifacts. You may select the same country or culture for each of the four popular culture artifacts.

Example:

Country or Culture: **France/French People**

Artifact: **The Dreamworks movie "Flushed Away"**

Depiction/Representation: **Although this is an animated film, there are a group of mercenary frogs that are hired to track the main characters when they flee from the main antagonist of the story. The French mercenary frogs are depicted as rude, foodies, avant-garde, and ethnocentric. The way they are depicted in this movie is not very inviting, and if I were to take these depictions as a real representation of French people and culture, I would have a negative image of both. I think this movie frames French people as snobbish and inherently judgmental toward cultures outside of France.**

Country: _____

Artifact: _____

_____

Depiction/Representation: _____

_____

_____

_____

_____

_____

_____

Country: _____

Artifact: _____

_____

Depiction/Representation: _____

_____

_____

_____

_____

_____

Country: _____

Artifact: _____

_____

Depiction/Representation: _____

_____

_____

_____

_____

_____

Country: _____

Artifact: _____

_____

Depiction/Representation: _____

_____

_____

_____

_____

_____

Name: _____   Period: _____

ICC Chapter 10 Activity Sheet #6

Top 10 Nonverbal Behaviors

Purchasing language software to study a foreign language is just a click away these days. Although some language software offers the equivalent of video clips identifying nonverbal behaviors, not enough emphasis is placed on the nonverbal component of communication. Communication scholars continue to call attention to the importance of nonverbal cues.

When traveling abroad, communicators need to be aware of what their nonverbal cues communicate to others. Nonverbal communication codes vary from culture to culture, so nonverbal behaviors can be interpreted very differently in different countries.

In the spaces provided below, identify a country you are interested in traveling to, and then note specific nonverbal practices or behaviors in this country of which you should be aware. General Internet searches, travel books, language guides and tutorials, cultural guides, and YouTube videos will yield tips about nonverbal communication in specific countries.

Example:

Country: **Japan**

Nonverbal Cue: **Waving one's hand in front of their nose back and forth**

Meaning: **In America, if a person were to wave their hand back and forth in front of their nose people would assume that there was an unpleasant odor somewhere in the vicinity. When communicating in Japan and doing this motion, it simply means no or no thank you. Of course there is a time and place to use such a gesture, but it is not considered rude to use when answering certain types of questions.**

Country: _____

Nonverbal Cue #1: _____

_____

Meaning: _____

_____

_____

_____

_____

_____

_____

Nonverbal Cue #2: _____

_____

Meaning: _____

_____

_____

_____

_____

Nonverbal Cue #3: _____

Meaning: _____

_____

_____

_____

_____

Nonverbal Cue #4: _____

Meaning: _____

_____

_____

_____

_____

Nonverbal Cue #5: _____

_____

Meaning: _____

_____

_____

_____

_____

_____

Nonverbal Cue #6: _____

_____

Meaning: _____

_____

_____

_____

_____

_____

Nonverbal Cue #7: _____

_____

Meaning: _____

_____

_____

_____

_____

_____

Nonverbal Cue #8: _____

_____

Meaning: _____

_____

_____

_____

_____

_____

Nonverbal Cue #9: _____

_____

Meaning: _____

_____

_____

_____

_____

_____

Nonverbal Cue #10: _____

_____

Meaning: _____

_____

_____

_____

_____

_____

Name: _____   Period: _____

ICC Chapter 10 Activity Sheet #7

Top 10 Words or Phrases

Most people will not have the time and resources needed to learn the languages of the international cultures they visit. Those who have an opportunity to learn a second language should definitely take it. For everyone else, it is important to recognize the language barrier and to take steps to improve your ability to communicate verbally with others while traveling or living abroad.

In the spaces provided below, identify 10 words or phrases from a country you are interested in traveling to, explain the meaning of the word or phrase, and explain why it is important. General Internet searches, travel books, language guides, language dictionaries, cultural guides, and YouTube videos can provide you with language tips.

Example:

Country: **South Korea** Language: **Korean**

Word or Phrase: **Ann-yeong-haseyo**

Meaning: **Hello**

Importance: **Although hello is a beginner's word for any language learner, sometimes it is the basics that help us set a solid foundation for communicating with others. Being able to say hello to others properly will enable me to do a number of things from the start of the interaction, including showing others that I am trying to learn Korean, but also that I am willing to put myself out there, and maybe they will take pity on me as I butcher other words I am struggling to pronounce correctly.**

Country: _____ Language: _____

Word or Phrase: _____

Meaning: _____

_____

_____

Importance: _____

_____

_____

_____

_____

Meaning: _____

_____

_____

Importance: _____

_____

_____

_____

_____

Word or Phrase: _____

Meaning: _____

_____

_____

Importance: _____

_____

_____

_____

_____

Word or Phrase: _____

Meaning: _____

_____

_____

Importance: _____

_____

_____

_____

_____

Word or Phrase: _____

Meaning: _____

_____

_____

_____

Importance: _____

_____

_____

_____

_____

_____

Word or Phrase: _____

Meaning: _____

_____

_____

Importance: _____

_____

_____

_____

_____

Word or Phrase: _____

Meaning: _____

_____

_____

Importance: _____

_____

_____

_____

_____

Word or Phrase: _____

Meaning: _____

_____

_____

_____

Importance: _____

_____

_____

_____

_____

Word or Phrase: _____

Meaning: _____

_____

_____

Importance: _____

_____

_____

_____

Word or Phrase: _____

Meaning: _____

_____

Importance: _____

_____

_____

_____

_____

Name: _____   Period: _____

ICC Chapter 10 Activity Sheet #8

Bridging the Gap Between Health Professionals and Patients

Identify some of the *health* and *communication* issues that may arise when a healthcare professional is not familiar with the needs and/or reality of a patient that belongs to a minority group or whose experiences are *different* from the norm, dominant culture, or health professional's own experiences.

The Scenario	The Problem	Bridge the Gap—How could the health professional bridge the gap? How could the patient bridge the gap?
Anna is a lesbian woman unsure about how to explain to her gynecologist that although she is sexually active and does not want children she is not interested in birth control. Anna prefers not to disclose her sexual identity because she fears being judged.		
Juan is a Spanish-speaking patient who wants to ask questions about his upcoming surgery but the interpreter doesn't seem to fully capture his concerns or convey instructions in a way that he can understand.		
John is a truck driver who has an irregular travel schedule and was diagnosed with cancer. John doesn't know how to explain to his doctor that the treatment prescribed, chemotherapy, is incompatible with his travel schedule. He needs his job to maintain health insurance and provide for his family.		
Juliana, a Brazilian immigrant, is unsatisfied that her son's pediatrician appointment in the United States is briefer and more superficial than in her homeland. Back in Brazil most of the appointment time was a physical examination conducted by the pediatrician, rather than a triage by medical assistants.		
Nancy is experiencing menopause but is tired of being told that menopause is the cause of all her problems. She is certain she is experiencing something else and being misdiagnosed, but health professionals have been dismissive.		
Joan is a young black physician who was told by her patient that she would like to be seen by someone else.		

Based on the insight gained through the scenarios above and your own personal experience, describe some of the risks involved when health professionals are culturally different from the people they serve. In your opinion, how can these risks best be minimized?

_____

_____

_____

_____

_____

_____

_____

_____

_____

_____

_____

_____

Chapter Evaluation

Name: _____

Chapter: _____

Class: _____

Most difficult or confusing ideas from the chapter:

1. _____

   _____

   _____

2. _____

   _____

   _____

Most controversial or hard to accept ideas from the chapter:

1. _____

   _____

   _____

2. _____

   _____

   _____

Suggestions for improving the chapter:

1. _____

   _____

   _____

2. _____

   _____

   _____

Most important or useful ideas from the chapter:

1. _____

_____

_____

2. _____

_____

_____

3. _____

_____

_____

Most important chapter skills and/or attitudes to develop:

1. _____

_____

_____

2. _____

_____

_____

Questions generated by reading the chapter:

1. _____

_____

_____

2. _____

_____

_____

CHAPTER QUIZ ANSWERS

Chapter 1

1. D.
2. B.
3. E.
4. A.
5. G.
6. C.
7. F.
8. H.
9. I.
10. D.
11. C.
12. B.
13. G.
14. F.
15. I.
16. A.
17. E.
18. H.
19. False.
    (Approx. 200)
20. True.
    ("co-culture" is more
    acceptable)
22. True.
23. False.
24. True.
25. True.
26. D.
27. B.
28. D.
29. D.
30. Edward T. Hall

Chapter 2

1. F.
2. E.
3. J.
4. K.
5. C.
6. L.
7. B.
8. G.
9. D.
10. A.
11. I.
12. H.
13. I.
14. L.
15. D.
16. C.
17. H.
18. E.
19. J.
20. G.
21. A.
22. K.
23. B.
24. F.
25. False.
    (reverse)
26. True.
27. cognitive restructuring
28. True.
29. False.
    (can unite people)
30. False.
    (ability to make fine
    distinctions)
31. False.
    (can be valid)
32. False.
    (still offensive)
33. False.
    (we prefer home)
34. False.
    (problematic)
35. culture shock

Chapter 3

1. D.
2. E.
3. B.
4. A.
5. C.
6. F.
7. H.
8. G.
9. J.
10. K.
11. A.
12. I.
13. L.
14. B.
15. H.
16. G.
17. C.
18. D.
19. F.
20. E.
21. assimilation
22. True.
23. False.
    (takes years)
24. False.
    (reverse)
25. False.
    (affective/cognitive)
26. perspective taking
27. True.
28. False.
    (also better health)
29. True.
30. True.
31. False.
    (more empathy)
32. True.
33. True.
34. False.
    (Golden Rule)
35. Emotional resilience

Chapter 4

1. F.
2. E.
3. D.
4. C.
5. G.
6. A.
7. B.
8. K.
9. J.
10. I.
11. H.
12. M.
13. N.
14. L.
15. D.
16. C.
17. A.
18. B.
19. False.
    (7,000)
20. True.
21. True.
22. True.
23. False.
    (reverse)
24. D.
25. False.
    (low context)
26. True.
27. taboo
28. True.
29. False.
30. False.
31. True.
32. False.
33. False.
    (14 languages)
34. False.
    (avoid idiomatics)
35. False.
    (apology is good)

Chapter 5

1. D.
2. G.
3. B.
4. E.
5. F.
6. H.
7. I.
8. K.
9. L.
10. J.
11. C.
12. A.
13. B.
14. G.
15. H.
16. D.
17. K.
18. L.
19. C.
20. A.
21. F.
22. E.
23. J.
24. I.
25. D.
26. C.
27. B.
28. A.
29. B.
30. False.
    (reverse)
31. E.
32. D.
33. inscrutability
34. relational
35. False.
    (ways to improve)

Chapter 6

1. D.
2. B.
3. G.
4. I.
5. J.
6. K.
7. F.
8. C.
9. H.
10. E.
11. L.
12. A.
13. C.
14. A.
15. B.
16. J.
17. L.
18. K.
19. I.
20. H.
21. G.
22. F.
23. E.
24. D.
25. True.
26. E.
27. True.
28. E.
29. True.
30. False.
    (monochronic)
31. face
32. False.
    (about 20)
33. False.
    (partial win/lose)
34. avoiding
35. discussion

Chapter 7

1. H.
2. F.
3. D.
4. G.
5. E.
6. K.
7. I.
8. J.
9. B.
10. A.
11. C.
12. C.
13. B.
14. A.
15. D.
16. G.
17. F.
18. E.
19. I.
20. H.
21. values
22. True.
23. benevolence
24. universalism
25. self-direction
26. True.
27. False.
    (six dimensions)
28. False.
    (reverse)
29. True.
30. worldview
31. E. All of the above.
32. True.
33. D.
34. True.
35. C.

Chapter 8

1. C.
2. E.
3. D.
4. F.
5. G.
6. B.
7. A.
8. H.
9. L.
10. K.
11. M.
12. J.
13. I.
14. True.
15. False.
16. False.
17. True.
18. E.
19. E.
20. True.
21. False.
    (white males)
22. True.
23. True.
24. diaspora
25. False.
    (five)
26. True.
27. False.
    (confusion)
28. True.
29. True.
30. True.

Chapter 9

1. C.
2. E.
3. D.
4. F.
5. B.
6. G.
7. K.
8. I.
9. J.
10. H.
11. A.
12. True.
13. True.
14. False.
    (changes over time)
15. True.
16. E.
17. E.
18. True.
19. True.
20. True.
21. True.
22. False.
    (only one)
23. prejudice
24. privilege
25. True.
26. C.
27. B.
28. A.
29. D.
30. True.

Chapter 10

1. D.
2. M.
3. N.
4. G.
5. H.
6. O.
7. I.
8. A.
9. F.
10. J.
11. K.
12. L.
13. B.
14. C.
15. E.
16. False.
    (See #17.)
17. True.
18. False.
    (not initially)
19. True.
20. False.
21. xenophobia
22. responsible
23. E.
24. Peace Corps
25. False.
26. False.
    (1 in 6)
27. True.
28. E.
29. D.
30. Romeo and Juliet
31. True.
32. False.
33. True.
34. False.
    (communication is
    a transaction)
35. True.